India after Alexander

Also by the author:
Vedic Physics: Scientific Origin of Hinduism
India before Alexander: A New Chronology
India after Vikramāditya: The Melting Pot

India after Alexander

The Age of Vikramādityas

Raja Ram Mohan Roy, Ph.D.

Mount Meru Publishing

Published in 2015 by:
Mount Meru publishing
P.O. Box 30026
Cityside Postal Outlet PO
Mississauga, Ontario
Canada L4Z 0B6
Email: mountmerupublishing@gmail.com

ISBN 978-0-9684120-6-0

Dedicated to Netaji Subhas Chandra Bose (1897-?) – patriot, nationalist, hero -- brave efforts made India independent.

CONTENTS

PREFACE

As a young man, I had promised myself to critically examine the evidence used to write a divisive history of India. Critical thinking is much needed in our mundane life as much as in the realm of scholarly work. At the very basic level, critical thinking is the ability to separate facts from fancies, and the willingness to analyze the raw data to arrive at independent, well-thought-out conclusions. I have applied this tool to Indian history in my books. It can as well be applied to the field of religion. Sadly, most people don't do that, even the ones who are capable of critical thinking. People are prone to believe anything in the name of religion, which otherwise they will consider utterly ridiculous. Historians need to apply critical thinking in the analysis of religion in order to get a true picture of history. I hope to delve deeper into these matters in my reconstruction of early Indian history, when religious doctrines were still getting formulated.

When I started my work on the reconstruction of Indian history, I had conceptualized writing a series of books presenting an alternative chronology that better explains available data. In my book "India before Alexander: A New Chronology", I have considered carefully the problems with currently accepted chronology, and identified the real person behind the adopted name of Devānāmpriya Priyadarśī, which opened the door for constructing an alternative chronology. In this book, I consider next the invasion of India by Alexander the Great. After presenting an in-depth discussion of what transpired in the aftermath of the battle between Alexander and Porus, I come to the crux of this book: a critical analysis of the beginning of various eras prevalent in Ancient India. Once we get a proper measure of how these eras were interrelated, we can begin placing various dynasties in their proper chronological/time slots. This book covers the period between the invasion of India by Alexander and the death of Emperor Vikramāditya in 57 BCE. This was an incredible period in Indian history, when the title of Vikramāditya was adopted by Gupta emperors, starting with Samudragupta. Over time the characters of different historical Vikramādityas merged with that of the legendary Vikramāditya creating a confusion of epic proportions. As a result, modern historians, who are trained to be skeptical of Hindu narratives, leveraged that confusion to deny the historicity of Emperor Vikramāditya. In this book the entangled fables have been separated and analyzed to establish the historicity of Emperor Vikramāditya in whose name the Vikrama Era was instituted.

I would like to thank Mr. Ramesh and Vimla Babbar for their encouragement and financial support towards publishing this book. I would also like to express my sincere gratitude to Prof. Ramesh Rao for editing the book.

Raja Ram Mohan Roy
Mississauga, Ontario, Canada
August 2015

TRANSLITERATION GUIDE

अ	a	आ	ā		
इ	i	ई	ī		
उ	u	ऊ	ū	ऋ	ṛ
ए	e	ऐ	ai		
ओ	o	औ	au		
अं	ṃ	अः	ḥ		
क	k	ख	kh		
ग	g	घ	gh	ङ	ṅ
च	ch*	छ	chh*		
ज	j	झ	jh	ञ	ñ
ट	ṭ	ठ	ṭh		
ड	ḍ	ढ	ḍh	ण	ṇ
त	t	थ	th		
द	d	ध	dh	न	n
प	p	फ	ph		
ब	b	भ	bh	म	m
य	y	र	r		
ल	l	व	v		
श	ś	ष	ṣ	स	s
ह	h	क्ष	kṣ	त्र	tr
ज्ञ	jñ	श्र	śr		

*Slightly different from International Alphabet of Sanskrit Transliteration scheme.

"Violence can only be concealed by a lie, and the lie can only be maintained by violence."

- Aleksandr Solzhenitsyn

1. IN THE DEAD OF THE NIGHT

The history of Alexander's invasion of India is known mainly through the Greek historians. There is no report from the Indian side regarding his battle with Porus. When there is information available from only one side, historians need to be extremely careful in arriving at conclusions as bias is inherent in such one-sided accounts. What happened during the battle been Alexander and Porus? Was Alexander really magnanimous after the battle? Have Greek historians lied regarding the outcome of this famous battle? Let us look carefully at and critically examine the available evidence.

1.1 Sources of Information

The information from Greek sources regarding the invasion of India by Alexander has been compiled together in "The Invasion of India by Alexander the Great" by John W. McCrindle, who relied on the following works for his compilation [1]:

- "The Anabasis of Alexander," by Arrian of Nikomedeia
- "The History of Alexander the Great," by Quintus Curtius Rufus
- "The Life of Alexander," in Plutarch's "Parallel Lives"

- "The History," by Diodoros the Sicilian
- "The Book of Macedonian History," compiled from the "Universal History of Trogus Pompeius," by Justinus Frontinus.

McCrindle gives the following information about the date of these Greek historians [2]:

> *"Arrian, who is universally allowed to be by far the best of all Alexander's historians, was at once a philosopher, a statesman, a military commander, an expert in the tactics of war, and an accomplished writer. He was born towards the end of the first century of our era at Nikomedeia (now Ismiknid or Ismid), the capital of Bithynia, situated near the head of a deep bay at the south-eastern end of the Propontis or Sea of Marmora....*
>
> *Nothing is known with any certainty respecting either the life of this historian (Curtius) or the time at which he lived. ... The materials of his narrative were drawn chiefly from Ptolemy, who accompanied Alexander into India....*
>
> *Plutarch was a native of Chaironeia, a town in Boiotia. The date of his birth is unknown, but may be fixed towards the middle of the first century of our era....*
>
> *Diodoros was born at Agyrium, a city in the interior of Sicily, and was a contemporary of Julius Caesar and the Emperor Augustus....*
>
> *As the earliest writer by whom he (Justinus Frontinus) is mentioned is St. Jerome, his date cannot be later than the beginning of the fifth century of our era."*

1.2 Encounter with Indian Philosophers

Before we go into the details of Alexander's invasion, it is interesting to know what Indian philosophers thought of Alexander, when they encountered him [3]:

"I commend the Indian sages of whom it is related that certain of them who had been caught by Alexander walking about according to their wont in the open meadow, did nothing else in sight of himself and his army but stamp upon the ground on which they were stepping. When he asked them through interpreters what they meant by so doing, they replied thus: O King Alexander, each man possesses as much of the earth as what we have stepped on; but you, being a man like the rest of us, except that you wickedly disturb the peace of' the world, have come so far from home to plague yourself and everyone else, and yet ere long when you die you will possess just so much of the earth as will suffice to make a grave to cover your bones. Alexander praised what they had said, but nevertheless continued to act in opposition to their advice. ... When he arrived at Taxila and saw the Indian gymnosophists, he conceived a great desire that one of their number should live with him, because he admired their patience in enduring hardships. But the oldest of the philosophers, Dandamis by name, with whom the others lived as disciples, not only refused to go himself, but forbade the others to go. He is said to have replied that he was also a son of Zeus, if Alexander was such (Referring to the terms in which he was summoned to go to Alexander. He was to go to "the son of Zeus."), and that he wanted nothing that was Alexander's; for he was content with what he had, while he saw that the men with Alexander wandered over sea and land for no advantage, and were never coming to an end of their wanderings. He desired, therefore, nothing it was in Alexander's power to give: nor did he fear being excluded from anything he possessed; for while he lived, India would suffice for him, yielding him her fruits in due season, and when he died he would be delivered from the body an unsuitable companion. Alexander accordingly did not attempt to compel him to go with him, considering him free to please himself. But Megasthenes has stated that Kalanos, one of the philosophers of this place, was persuaded to go since he had no power of self-control, as the philosophers themselves allowed, who upbraided him

because he had deserted the happiness among them, and went to serve another master than the deity."

1.3 Between Indus and Hydaspes

As Alexander moved towards India, the ruler of the region east of the Indus called variously Taxiles, Omphis and Mophis by Greek writers surrendered meekly, as described by Arrian, Curtius and Diodorus. Here are some relevant passages:

Arrian: "When spring was now past (the spring of 327 B.C.), he led his army from Baktra to invade the Indians, ... Having reached the city of Nikaia and sacrificed to the goddess Athena, he dispatched a herald to Taxiles and the chiefs on this side of the river Indus, directing them to meet him where it was most convenient for each. Taxiles accordingly and the other chiefs did meet him and brought him such presents as are most esteemed by the Indians. They offered also to give him the elephants which they had with them amounting in number to five-and-twenty." [4]

Arrian; "When Alexander arrived at the river Indus he found a bridge already made over it by Hephaistion, and two thirty-oared galleys, besides a great many small boats. He found also a present which had been sent by Taxiles the Indian, consisting of 200 talents of silver, 3000 oxen fattened for the shambles, 10,000 sheep or more, and 30 elephants. The same prince had also sent to his assistance a force of 700 horsemen, and these brought word that Taxiles surrendered into his hands his capital Taxila, the greatest of all the cities between the river Indus and the Hydaspes." [5]

Arrian: "When Alexander had crossed to the other side of the Indus he again offered sacrifice according to his custom. Then marching away from the Indus he arrived at Taxila, a great and flourishing city, the greatest indeed of all the cities which lay between the river Indus and the Hydaspes. Taxiles, the governor of the city, and the Indians who belonged to it received him in a friendly manner, and he therefore added as much of the adjacent country to their territory as they requested. While he was there Abisares, the king of the Indians of the hill-country, sent him an embassy which included his own brother and other grandees of his court. Envoys came also from Doxares, the chief of the province, and those like the others brought presents." [6]

Curtius: "The sovereign of the territories on the other side was Omphis; who had urged his father to surrender his kingdom to Alexander, and had moreover at his father's death sent envoys to enquire whether it was Alexander's pleasure that he should meanwhile exercise authority or remain in a private capacity till his arrival. ... then the barbarian prince explained that he had come with his army to meet Alexander that he might at once place at his disposal all the forces of his empire, without waiting to tender his allegiance through deputies. He surrendered, he said, his person and his kingdom to a man who, as he knew, was fighting not more for fame than fearing to incur the reproach of perfidy." [7]

Diodorus: "For Taxiles being by this time dead, his son Mophis had succeeded to the government. Now Mophis had before this not only sent word to Alexander, then in Sogdiana, that he would fight on his side against any Indians who might appear in arms against him, but at this juncture had also sent ambassadors to say that he surrendered his kingdom into his hands. So when Alexander was at a distance of forty stadia he set forth to meet him, attended by his friends ..." [8]

1.4 The Encounter with Porus

Taxiles ruled over a region between the rivers Indus and Hydaspes. The current name of Hydaspes is Jhelum and its ancient name was Vitastā. Beyond Hydaspes a fearless warrior king named Porus was ready and waiting to defend his kingdom at any cost. Here is how Curtius describes the state of preparedness of Porus [9]:

"When Alexander asked him whether he had more husbandmen or soldiers, he replied that as he was at war with two kings he required

> *more soldiers than field labourers. These kings were Abisares and Porus, but Porus was superior in power and influence. Both of them held sway beyond the river Hydaspes, and had resolved to try the fortune of war whatever invader might come. ... Alexander, thinking that by the mere prestige of his name Porus also would be induced to surrender, sent Cleochares to tell him in peremptory terms that he must pay tribute and come to meet his sovereign at the very frontiers of his own dominions. Porus answered that he would comply with the second of these demands, and when Alexander entered his realm he would meet him, but come armed for battle. ... Alexander having then put the traitor and his accomplice under custody, and consigned the elephants to the care of Taxiles, advanced till he reached the river Hydaspes, where on the further bank Porus had encamped to prevent the enemy from landing. In the van of his army he had posted 85 elephants of the greatest size and strength, and behind these 300 chariots and somewhere about 30,000 infantry, among whom were the archers, whose arrows, as already stated, were too ponderous to be readily discharged. He was himself mounted on an elephant which towered above all its fellows, while his armour, embellished with gold and silver, set off his supremely majestic person to great advantage. His courage matched his bodily vigour, and his wisdom was the utmost attainable in a rude community."*

1.5 The War Games

It was not easy for Alexander to cross Hydaspes with his army under the watch of Porus. Alexander tried to fool Porus by manoeuvring his troops, but did not succeed completely. Arrian has described the movement of Alexander's troops in the following words [10]:

> *"Alexander encamped on the banks of the river, and Poros was seen on the opposite side, with all his army and his array of elephants around him. Against the place where he saw Alexander had encamped, he remained himself to guard the passage, but he sent*

detachments of his men, each commanded by a captain, to guard all parts of the river where it could be easily forded, as he was resolved to prevent the Macedonians from effecting a landing. When Alexander saw this, he thought it expedient to move his army from place to place, so that Poros might be at a loss to discover his real intentions. For this purpose he divided his army into many parts, and some of the troops he led himself in different directions, sometimes to ravage the enemy's country, and sometimes to find out where he could most easily ford the river. He placed various commanders at various times over different divisions of his army, and dispatched them also in different directions. At the same time he caused provisions to be conveyed to the camp from all parts of the country on this side of the river, to impress Poros with the conviction that he intended to remain where he was near the bank, till the waters of the river subsided in winter, and afforded him a large choice of passages. As the boats were constantly plying up and down the stream, and the skins were being filled with hay, while all the bank was lined, here with horse and there with foot, all this prevented Poros from resting and concentrating his preparations at anyone point selected in preference to any other as the best for defending the passage. At this time of the year besides, all the Indian rivers were swollen and flowing with turbid and rapid currents, for the sun is then wont to turn towards the summer tropic. At this season incessant rains deluge the soil of India, and the snows of the Kaukasos then melting flood the numerous rivers to which they give birth. ... Alexander therefore publicly announced that he would remain where he was throughout that season of the year if his passage was for the present to be obstructed, but he continued as before waiting in ambush to see whether he could anywhere rapidly steal a passage to the other side without being observed. He clearly saw that it was impossible for him to cross where Poros himself had encamped near the bank of the Hydaspes, not only because he had so many elephants, but also because his large army arrayed for battle, and splendidly accoutered, was ready to attack his troops the moment they landed. He foresaw besides that his horses would refuse to mount the opposite bank, where the elephants would at once encounter them, and by their very aspect and their roaring would terrify them outright; nor did he think that even before they gained the shore they would remain upon the inflated hides during the passage; but that on seeing the elephants even at a distance off, they would become frantic and leap into the water. He resolved therefore to steal the passage, and to do this in the following way. Leading out by night the greater part of his cavalry along the river bank in different directions, he ordered them to set up a loud clamour, raise the war-shout,[1] and fill the shores with every kind of noise, as if they were really preparing to attempt the passage. Poros marched meanwhile along the opposite bank, in the direction of the noise, having his elephants with him, and Alexander gradually accustomed him to lead out his men in this way in opposition. When this had been done repeatedly, and the men did nothing more than make a great noise and shout the war-cry, Poros no longer made any counter-movement when the cavalry issued out from the camp, but remained within his own lines, his spies being, however, posted at numerous points along the bank. … Alexander himself embarked on a thirty-oared galley, and went over accompanied by Ptolemy, Perdikkas, and Lysimachos, his body-guards, and by Seleukos, one of the companions, who was afterwards king, and by one half of the hypaspists, the other half being on board of the other galleys of like size. As soon as the soldiers had passed beyond the island, they steered for the bank, being now full in view of the enemy, whose sentinels on seeing their approach galloped off at the utmost speed of each man's horse to carry the tidings to Poros."

1.6 The Battle of the Hydaspes

Finally, the armies of Alexander and Porus charged against each other on the banks of the Hydaspes. Plutarch has described the famous battle of the Hydaspes in the following words [11]:

"At last, upon a dark and stormy night, he took a part of the infantry and a choice body of cavalry, marched to a considerable distance from the enemy, and crossed over to an island of no great size. Here he was exposed with his army to the rage of a violent thunderstorm, amid which rain fell down in torrents, and though he saw some of his men struck dead with the lightning, he nevertheless advanced from the island and reached the furthermost bank of the river. The Hydaspes was now flooded by the rains, and its raging current had chosen a new channel of great width, down which a great body of water was carried. In fording this new bed, he could with difficulty keep his footing, as the bottom was very slippery and uneven. It was here that Alexander is said to have exclaimed, "0 Athenians! can you believe what dangers I undergo to earn your applause?" This particular rests on the authority of Onesikritos, for Alexander himself merely says that he and his men left their rafts, and under arms waded through the second torrent with the water up to their breasts. After crossing, he himself rode forward about twenty stadia in advance of the infantry, concluding that if the enemy attacked him with their cavalry only, he could easily rout them; but if they moved forward their entire force, he could bring his infantry into the field before fighting began. He was right in both conclusions, for he fell in with 1000 horse and 60 war-chariots of the enemy, and these he routed, capturing every chariot, and slaying 400 of the horsemen. Poros thus perceived that Alexander himself had crossed the river, and he therefore advanced against him with all his army, except some troops which he left to guard his camp, in case the Macedonians should cross from the opposite bank to attack it. Alexander, dreading the elephants and the great numbers of the enemy, did not engage with them in front, but attacked them himself on the left wing, ordering Koinos to fall upon them on the right. Both wings were broken, and the enemy, driven from their position, thronged always towards the centre where the elephants were posted. The contest, which began early in the morning, was so obstinately maintained that it was fully the eighth hour of the day before the Indians renounced all attempts at further resistance. This

> *description of the battle is given by the chief actor in it himself in his letters. Most historians are agreed that Poros stood four cubits and a span high, and that his gigantic form was not less proportioned to the elephant which carried him, and which was his biggest, than was a rider of an ordinary size to his horse. This elephant showed wonderful sagacity and care for its royal master, for while it was still vigorous it defended him against his assailants and repulsed them, but when it perceived that he was ready to sink from the number of his wounds and bruises, fearing that he might fall off its back, it gently lowered itself to the ground, and as it knelt quietly extracted the darts from his body with its trunk. When Poros was taken prisoner, Alexander asked him how he wished to be treated. "Like a king," answered Poros. When Alexander further asked if he had anything else to request, "Everything," rejoined Poros, "is comprised in the words, like a king." Alexander then not only reinstated Poros in his kingdom with the title of satrap, but added a large province to it, subduing the inhabitants whose form of government was the republican. This country, it is said, contained 15 tribes, 5000 considerable cities, and villages without number."*

This is what we have read in history books. Is this what really happened that night? Let's take a critical look.

1.7 Did Alexander lose to Porus?

Marshal Georgi Zhukov was no ordinary man. He was the commander of the Russian Red Army, which pushed the Nazi army from Stalingrad all the way back to Berlin resulting in the collapse of the Nazi regime. He was the most successful Russian General during World War II and was known as the "man who did not lose a battle". When he was addressing the cadets of the Indian Military Academy, Dehradun in 1957, he said that Alexander had suffered an outright defeat during the Battle of Hydaspes. Here is an excerpt from the news report [12]:

"In Zhukov's view, Alexander had suffered a greater setback in India than Napoleon in Russia. Napoleon had invaded Russia with 600,000 troops; of these only 30,000 survived, and of that number fewer than 1,000 were ever able to return to duty. So if Zhukov was comparing Alexander's campaign in India to Napoleon's disaster, the Macedonians and Greeks must have retreated in an equally ignominious fashion. Zhukov would know a fleeing force if he saw one; he had chased the German Army over 2000 km from Stalingrad to Berlin."

Let me try to formulate the arguments in favour of Alexander's rout by Porus that would have prompted Zhukov to come to the shocking conclusion regarding the battle of the Hydaspes. Only when we critically analyze the pieces of evidence staring at us that we get to the truth.

1.7.1 If something is too good to be true, it probably is

We have heard about the magnanimity of Alexander after the battle of the Hydaspes. Arrian has described the outcome of this battle in the following words [13]:

"He was then conducted to Alexander, who, on learning that Meroes was approaching with him, rode forward in front of his line with a few of the Companions to meet him. Then reining in his horse he beheld with admiration the handsome person and majestic stature of Poros, which somewhat exceeded five cubits. He saw, too, with wonder that he did not seem to be broken and abased in spirit, but that he advanced to meet him as a brave man would meet another brave man after gallantly contending with another king in defence of his kingdom. Then Alexander, who was the first to speak, requested Poros to say how he wished to be treated. The report goes that Poros said in reply, "Treat me, O Alexander! as befits a king;" and that Alexander, being pleased with his answer, replied, "For mine own sake, O Poros! thou shalt be so treated, but do thou, in thine own behalf, ask for whatever boon thou pleasest," to which

> *Poros replied that in what he had asked everything was included. Alexander was more delighted than ever with this rejoinder, and not only appointed Poros to govern his own Indians, but added to his original territory another of still greater extent."*

Isn't this too good to be true? Is there any other example in the entire history of humanity when the vanquished has not only been returned his kingdom, but more territory has been added to his kingdom?

1.7.2 Alexander was a cruel man

In the documentary series "Ancients behaving Badly" that aired in 2009 on The History Channel, a number of historical figures have been evaluated by historians and psychiatrists for being "goal driven killers" to "psychopathic murderers". These historical figures included Caligula, Attila the Hun, Julius Caesar, Alexander the Great, Nero, Hannibal, Genghis Khan, and Cleopatra. To make it to the list is proof enough that Alexander was not such a nice person that he is made out to be.

Alexander has been accused of conspiring to get his father killed in order to ascend the throne [14]. He killed many of his close subordinates unjustly. According to Arrian, Hermolaus made the following accusations before his execution [15]:

> *"He then recounted all his acts of despotism, the illegal execution of Philotas, the still more illegal one of his father Parmenio and of others who were put to death at that time, the murder of Clitus in a fit of drunkenness, ... He said that, being no longer able to bear these things, he wished to free both himself and other Macedonians."*

McCrindle has described the execution of Philotas in the following words [16]:

> *"Here an event occurred which has left a dark stain on the character of Alexander. He was led to suspect that a conspiracy had been*

formed against his life by some of his principal officers, and among others by the son of Parmenion, Philotas, who held the most coveted post in the army, that of commander of the Companion Cavalry. It is certain that he was not an accomplice in the plot; but as he had been informed of its existence, and failed to give the king any warning of his danger, he was accused before the Macedonian army and condemned to death. He confessed under torture that his father, Parmenion, had formed a design against the king's life, and that he had himself joined the recent plot, lest his father, who was now an old man, might, before the plot was ripe, be snatched away by death from his command at Ekbatana, which placed the vast treasures deposited there at his disposal. This confession, wrung by torture when its agonies became insupportable, and obviously framed to meet the wishes of the questioners, was no proof of the guilt either of the father or the son. Parmenion was, nevertheless, on this worthless evidence condemned to death, and Alexander, whom he had so faithfully served, took care that the sentence should be executed before the news of his son's death, which he might seek to avenge, could reach his ears. Many other Macedonians were also at this time tried and put to death."

The treatment of Bessus by Alexander is even more horrific. Arrian had described the inhuman treatment of Bessus by Alexander in the following words [17]:

"Then Alexander gathered a conference of those who were then at hand, and led Bessus in before them. Having accused him of the betrayal of Darius, he ordered his nose and ears to be cut off, and that he should be taken to Ecbatana to be put to death there in the council of the Medes and Persians. . . . ."

Alexander even violated his own treaty by killing a number of people defending the town of Massaga after granting them immunity. Diodorus describes this massacre in the following words [18]:

"When the capitulation on those terms had been ratified by oaths,

the Queen [of Massaga], to show her admiration of Alexander's magnanimity, sent out to him most valuable presents, with an intimation that she would fulfill all the stipulations. Then the mercenaries at once, in accordance with the terms of the agreement, evacuated the city, and after retiring to a distance of eighty stadia, pitched their camp unmolested without thought of what was to happen. But Alexander, who was actuated by an implacable enmity against the mercenaries, and had kept his troops under arms ready for action, pursued the barbarians, and falling suddenly upon them, made a great slaughter of their ranks. The barbarians at first loudly protested that they were attacked in violation of sworn obligations, and invoked the gods whom he had desecrated by taking false oaths in their name. But Alexander with loud voice retorted that his covenant merely bound him to let them depart from the city, and was by no means a league of perpetual amity between them and the Macedonians. The mercenaries, undismayed by the greatness of their danger, drew their ranks together in form of a ring, within which they placed the women and children to guard them on all sides against their assailants. As they were now desperate, and by their audacity and feats of valour, made the conflict in which they closed hot work for the enemy, while the Macedonians held it a point of honour not to be outdone in courage by a horde of barbarians, great was the astonishment and alarm which the peril of the crisis created. For as the combatants were locked together fighting hand to hand, death and wounds were dealt round in every variety of form. Thus the Macedonians, when once their long spikes had shattered the shields of the barbarians, pierced their vitals with the steel points of these weapons, and on the other hand the mercenaries never hurled their javelins without deadly effect against the near mark presented by the dense ranks of the enemy. When many were thus wounded and not a few killed, the women, taking the arms of the fallen, fought side by side with the men, for the imminence of the danger and the great interests at stake forced them to do violence to their nature, and to take an active part in the defence. Accordingly some of them who had supplied themselves with arms, did their best to cover their husbands with their shields, while others who were without arms did much to impede the enemy by flinging themselves upon them and catching hold of their shields. The defenders, however, after fighting desperately along with their wives, were at last overpowered by superior numbers, and met a glorious death which they would have disdained to exchange for a life with dishonour."

1.7.3 Alexander never showed kindness to anyone who opposed him

We are told that Alexander was very kind to Porus because he was very impressed by his bravery. However, Alexander had never shown any kindness to anyone who had opposed him. Here are some quotes to this effect:

Diodoros: "He took many other cities, and put to death all who offered resistance to his arms." [19]

"To resist Alexander was to incur his wrath regardless of your religious beliefs, cultural persuasion, or ethnic identity. Throughout his military operations, Alexander followed a policy of rewarding those who surrendered quickly and punishing severely those who resisted. The classic example of the latter was his destruction of the rebellious city of Thebes, one of the great cities of Hellenic civilization." [20]

"The cities along the Syrian coast submitted in like manner to Alexander himself, all but Tyre, which sent him a golden crown, but refused to admit him within her gates. For this temerity the city of merchant princes paid a dreadful penalty. Alexander, having captured it after a seven months' siege, burned it to the ground, and most of the inhabitants he either slew or sold into slavery. This is considered to have been the greatest of all Alexander's military achievements. Tyre had hitherto been deemed impregnable. It was built on an island separated from the mainland by a channel of the sea half a mile in width; its walls, which were of great solidity, rose

> *to an immense height, and its navy gave it the command of the sea. The inhabitants, moreover, were expert in arms, and defended themselves with such spirit and obstinacy that Alexander found himself unable to overcome their resistance, until he obtained from Cyprus and Sidon a fleet superior to their own. He had also to construct a causeway through the channel to enable him to bring his engines close up to the walls, and this was a work of vast labour and difficulty. His merciless treatment of the vanquished darkly overshadows the glory of this memorable exploit."* [21]

If Alexander was never kind to people resisting him, how could he suddenly become so kind to Porus?

1.7.4 An army has never refused to fight in history

We have been told by Greek historians that Alexander's army refused to fight after the battle with Porus, even though Alexander wanted to go ahead and invade the interior parts of India. Here is what Plutarch has said [22]:

> *"The battle with Poros depressed the spirits of the Macedonians, and made them very unwilling to advance farther into India. For as it was with the utmost difficulty they had beaten him when the army he led amounted only to 20,000 infantry and 2000 cavalry, they now most resolutely opposed Alexander when he insisted that they should cross the Ganges."*

This was the supposed to have been such a tough battle that Alexander's army could not take it anymore. But if we take the words of Arrian, who is supposed to be the most reliable among Greek historians, there was hardly any fight [23]:

> *"The loss of the Indians in killed fell little short of 20,000 infantry and 3000 cavalry, and all their chariots were broken to pieces. Two sons of Poros fell in the battle, and also Spitakes, the chief of the Indians of that district. The drivers of the elephants and of the chariots were also slain and the cavalry officers and the generals in*

> *the army of Poros all ... On Alexander's side there fell about 80 of the 6000 infantry who had taken part in the first attack, 10 of the horse archers who first began the action, 20 of the companion cavalry, and 200 of the other cavalry."*

Does it look like a fight at all? This seems more like a cakewalk. If these are the real figures of the casualties on Alexander's side compared to Porus' side, Alexander's army should have been raring to go further. They did not and there is only one sane reason for that: because they could not. Never before in history and that includes not just up to Alexander's time, but up to our time, an army has refused to fight. In ancient times the soldiers would be executed and, now, they would be court-martialed. Armies have never had a choice in fighting anywhere in the world. It was always up to the ruler/leader to decide. We can therefore surmise that Greek historians cooked up an elaborate excuse to hide the real outcome of the battle.

1.7.5 Alexander was at a clear disadvantage

If Alexander and his army tried to cross the river Hydaspes, Porus was ready to attack them even before they could land on the other side. This is what Arrian has said [24]:

> *"Having appointed Philip, the son of Makhatas, satrap of the Indians of that district, he left a garrison in Taxila and those soldiers who were invalided, and then moved on towards the river Hydaspes - for he had learned that Porus with the whole of his army lay on the other side of that river resolved either to prevent him from making the passage or* ***to attack him when crossing****."*

On the other hand it was not easy to cross the Hydaspes at that time of the year, as told by Curtius [25]:

> *"The Macedonians were intimidated not only by the appearance of the enemy, but by the magnitude of the river to be crossed, which, spreading out to a width of no less than four stadia in a deep*

channel which nowhere opened a passage by fords, presented the aspect of a vast sea. Yet its rapidity did not diminish in proportion to its wider diffusion, but it rushed impetuously like a seething torrent compressed into a narrow bed by the closing in of its banks. Besides, at many points the presence of sunken rocks was revealed where the waves were driven back in eddies. The bank presented a still more formidable aspect, for, as far as the eye could see, it was covered with cavalry and infantry, in the midst of which, like so many massive structures, stood the huge elephants, which, being of set purpose provoked by their drivers, distressed the ear with their frightful roars. The enemy and the river both in their front, struck with sudden dismay the hearts of the Macedonians, disposed though they were to entertain good hopes, and knowing from experience against what fearful odds they had ere now contended. They could not believe that boats so unhandy could be steered to the bank or gain it in safety."

The situation was even worse on the night of the crossing, as told by Plutarch [26]:

"At last, upon a dark and stormy night, he took a part of the infantry and a choice body of cavalry, marched to a considerable distance from the enemy, and crossed over to an island of no great size. Here he was exposed with his army to the rage of a violent thunderstorm, amid which rain fell down in torrents, and though he saw some of his men struck dead with the lightning, he nevertheless advanced from the island and reached the furthermost bank of the river. The Hydaspes was now flooded by the rains, and its raging current had chosen a new channel of great width, down which a great body of water was carried. In fording this new bed, he could with difficulty keep his footing, as the bottom was very slippery and uneven."

Under these circumstances, when crossing the Hydaspes was itself so fraught with danger, how was an army going to cross the river and then fight an enemy, who was ready on guard and determined not to let them cross the river? Alexander had crossed the river surreptitiously with a small battalion, but was already spotted during crossing. Most of his army had to cross right before the watchful eyes of Porus. Was he just going to sit and watch while they tried to cross the river?

1.7.6 Alexander kept sending emissaries to Porus

If Porus was losing the battle, then why was Alexander so anxious to send emissary after emissary to ask Porus to stop fighting? This is exactly what Arrian has told us [27]:

> *"When he found himself wounded he turned his elephant round and began to retire. Alexander, perceiving that he was a great man and valiant in fight, was anxious to save his life, and for this purpose sent to him first of all Taxiles the Indian. Taxiles, who was on horseback, approached as near the elephant which carried Poros as seemed safe, and entreated him, since it was no longer possible for him to flee, to stop his elephant and listen to the message he brought from Alexander. But Poros, on finding that the speaker was his old enemy Taxiles, turned round and prepared to smite him with his javelin; and he would probably have killed him had not Taxiles instantly put his horse to the gallop and got beyond the reach of Poros. But not even for this act did Alexander feel any resentment against Poros,* ***but sent to him messenger after messenger****, and last of all Meroes, an Indian, as he had learned that Poros and this Meroes were old friends. As soon as Poros heard the message which Meroes now brought just at a time when he was overpowered by thirst, he made his elephant halt and dismounted. Then, when he had taken a draught of water and felt revived, he requested Meroes to conduct him without delay to Alexander."*

It is hard to imagine why Alexander would have been anxious to save the life of Porus. It would only make sense if Alexander was losing the battle badly and was anxious to stop fighting.

1.7.7 Taxiles made no gains from the defeat of Porus

Taxiles had cooperated with Alexander in the hope of settling his score with Porus with whom he had enmity. However, for all his support, including taking part in the battle against Porus, Taxiles seems to have gained nothing in return from Alexander. He might have even been forced to give his daughter in marriage to Porus. Here is what Curtius has said [28]:

> *"Designing now to make for the ocean with a thousand ships, he left Porus and Taxiles, the Indian kings who had been disagreeing and raking up old feuds, in friendly relations with each other, strengthened by a marriage alliance; and as they had done their utmost to help him forward with the building of his fleet, he confirmed each in his sovereignty."*

Alexander gave all the regions he had conquered to Porus. Taxiles was simply sent back to his capital with nothing to show for his loyalty. Here is what Arrian has said [29]:

> *"In this manner he took seven-and-thirty cities, the smallest of which contained not fewer than 5000 inhabitants, while many contained upwards of 10,000. He took also a great many villages which were not less populous than the towns; and this country he gave to Poros to rule, and between him and Taxiles he effected a reconciliation. He then sent Taxiles home to his capital."*

1.7.8 Alexander did not avenge the loss of his dear horse Boukephalos in the battle

According to Diodoros, Alexander's horse Boukephala died in the battle with Porus [30]:

> *"When the equipment of the fleet was finished, and 200 boats without hatches and 800 tenders had been got ready, he proceeded to give names to the cities which had been founded on the banks of the river, calling one Nikaia in commemoration of his victory, and*

> *the other Boukephala after his horse that perished in the battle with Poros."*

Curtius has also confirmed the death of Alexander's horse during the battle with Porus [31]:

> *"Alexander pursued, but his horse being pierced with many wounds fainted under him, and sank to the ground, laying the king down gently rather than throwing him from his seat."*

McCrindle makes the following comments on this statement by Curtius [32]:

> *"Regarding this horse it seems worth recording that when caparisoned and armed for battle he would not suffer himself to be mounted by anyone but the king. It is also told of this horse that in the Indian war when Alexander, mounted upon him, and performing noble deeds of bravery, had with too little heed for his own safety entangled himself amid a battalion of the enemy, where he was on all sides assailed with darts, his horse was stabbed with deep wounds in the neck and sides. Ready to expire, and drained of nearly all his blood, he nevertheless bore back the king from the midst of his foes at a most rapid pace; and when he had conveyed him beyond reach of spears, he straightway dropped down, and having no further fear for his master's safety, he breathed his last as if with the consolation of human sensibility. Then King Alexander having gained the victory in this war, built a town on this spot, and in honour of his horse called it Bucephalon."*

Greek writers have tried to twist the outcome of the battle, but have clearly failed to hide it. It was Alexander who was surrounded by enemies from all sides and attacked. He was injured badly himself and his horse barely managed to take him to safety. It follows then that it was Alexander who was sending messengers after messengers to Porus to stop the battle. If Porus had lost the battle in which Alexander's horse had died, there was no way Alexander would have left Porus alive. Arrian has told us that

Alexander was going to kill all Ouxians when his horse Boukephalas went missing [33]:

> *"This Boukephalas was never mounted by anyone except Alexander only, for he disdained all other riders. He was of uncommon size and of generous mettle. He had by way of a distinguishing mark the head of an ox impressed upon him, and some say that from this circumstance he got his name. But others say that though he was black, he had on his forehead a white mark which bore a close resemblance to the brow of an ox. In the country of the Ouxians this horse disappeared from Alexander, who sent a proclamation through the land that he would kill all the Ouxians if they did not bring him his horse, and brought back he was immediately after the proclamation had been issued - so great was Alexander's attachment to his favourite, and so great was the fear of Alexander which prevailed among the barbarians."*

1.7.9 Alexander did not return by the land route

When Alexander had decided that he was not going any further, he did not return by the land route he had taken to come to India. A victor would have gone back celebrating. Instead he went back through unchartered territory endangering the lives of his army. The reason is clear. He was not allowed to go back using the land route by Porus. Porus was not only a great warrior, but also a very strategic thinker. He figured out that if he let Alexander go back across the Hydaspes, Alexander was simply going to strengthen his army and come back to avenge his defeat. Instead, Porus gave him the only option, which was certain to diminish if not ruin his power.

1.7.10 Alexander took an unknown perilous route back through the Hydaspes and the Indus rivers to sea

Alexander had to go back by sailing through Hydaspes first and then through the Indus river. It took his army months to cut trees and build the fleet for this purpose. Here is what Greek writer Strabo has written [34]:

> *"Between the Hydaspes and Akesines is the country of Poros – an extensive and fertile district containing somewhere about 300 cities. Here in the neighbourhood of the Emodoi mountains is the forest where Alexander cut a great quantity of pine, fir, cedar and various other trees fit for shipbuilding. This timber he brought down the Hydaspes, and with it constructed a fleet on that river ...."*

Why would Alexander's army take up so much work, when they were too tired to fight according to the story made up to justify not going any further into India? Why would they take a perilous route if Alexander had won the battle with Porus? Is it conceivable that the greatest military strategist of all times, who had travelled thousands of miles to reach the land of Porus, did not know what awaited him a few miles down the river if he took a journey through Hydaspes? Clearly, Alexander was left with no choice by Porus. As Porus had lost his son in the battle, obviously he was not in a charitable mood. Alexander had to take this perilous route knowing the danger fully well. Here is what had happened at the confluence of the Hydaspes and Indus rivers according to Curtius [35]:

> *"But the meeting of the rivers makes the waters swell in great billows like those of the ocean, and the navigable way is compressed into a narrow channel by extensive mud-banks kept continually shifting by the force of the confluent waters. When the waves, therefore, in thick succession dashed against the vessels, beating both on their prows and sides, the sailors were obliged to take in sail; but partly from their own flurry, and partly from the force of the currents, they were unable to execute their orders in time, and before the eyes of all two of the large ships were engulphed in the stream. The smaller craft, however, though they also were unmanageable, were driven on shore without sustaining injury. The ship which had the king himself on board was caught in eddies of*

the greatest violence, and by their force was irresistibly driven athwart and whirled onward without answering the helm. He had already stripped off his clothes preparatory to throwing himself into the river, while his friends were swimming about not far off ready to pick him up, but as it was evident that the danger was about equal whether he threw himself into the water or remained on board, the boatmen vied with each other in stretching to their oars, and made every exertion possible for human beings to force their vessel through the raging surges. It then seemed as though the waves were being cloven asunder, and as though the whirling eddies were retreating, and the ship was thus at length rescued from their grasp. It did not, however, gain the shore in safety, but was stranded on the nearest shallows. One would suppose that a war had been waged against the river."

Things went from bad to worse for Alexander's army as they continued further. They had to fight for their supplies and there seemed no end to their misery. Curtius continues with the following description [36]:

"They were now exposed to fierce nations that with their blood they might open for him a way to the ocean. They were dragged onward outside the range of the constellations and the sun of their own zone, and forced to go to places which nature meant to be hidden from mortal eyes. New enemies were forever springing up with arms ever new, and though they put them all to rout and flight, what reward awaited them? What but mists and darkness and unbroken night hovering over the abyss of ocean? What but a sea teeming with multitudes of frightful monsters-stagnating waters in which expiring nature has given way in despair?"

The king, troubled not by any fears for himself, but by the anxiety of the soldiers about their safety, called them together, and pointed out to them that those of whom they were afraid were weak and unwarlike; that after the conquest of these tribes there was nothing in their way, once they had traversed the distance now between them and the ocean, to prevent their coming to the end of the world, which would be also the end of their labours; that he had given way to their fears of the Ganges and of the numerous tribes beyond that river, and turned his arms to a quarter where the glory would be equal but the hazard less; that they were already in sight of the ocean, and were already fanned by breezes from the sea. They should not then grudge him the glory to which he aspired. They would over-pass the limits reached by Hercules and Father Bacchus, and thus at a small cost bestow upon their king an immortality of fame. They should permit him to return from India with honour, and not to escape from it like a fugitive."

There we have it as explicit as it can get. Alexander was himself begging his army to let him return with honour and not return like a fugitive. If this is not the admission of defeat in the battle, what else would be?

1.7.11 Alexander lost most of his army on the way back

When Alexander finally reached the sea, he divided his army and one division took the sea route while the rest followed the land route close to the sea through the desert of Gedrosia. Strabo has described this part of the journey in the following words [37]:

"Having made three divisions of his army, he advanced himself with one of them through Gedrosia, keeping at most a distance from the sea of 500 stadia, that he might make preparations along the coast for the benefit of his fleet. He was frequently in close proximity to the sea, although the beach was impracticable and rugged. The second division he sent on before him, under Krateros, through the interior, that he might reduce Ariane, while advancing to the places to which Alexander himself was directing his march. The fleet he entrusted to Nearchos and Onesikritos, the pilot-in-chief, instructing them to take up convenient positions as they followed him, and to sail along the coast parallel to his line of march. Nearchos relates that while Alexander was marching away from

India, he himself, in Autumn, about the time when the Pleiades rise after sunset, began his voyage, even though the winds were contrary, because the barbarians were attacking his troops and trying to drive them out of the country. They had waxed bold after the king's departure, and were bent on asserting their liberty. Krateros again settling out from the Hydaspes went through the country of the Arachotians and Drangians into Karmania. But Alexander suffered sorely all throughout his march, as his road lay through a miserably barren country. He was equally unfortunate in the matter of provisions, which were not only brought from a distance, but brought so seldom and in such small quantities, that the army suffered greatly from hunger, while the beasts of burden broke down, and the baggage was abandoned both on the march and in the camp. The army was indebted for its salvation to the dates and edible pith of the palm trees. Nearchos says that Alexander, being impressed with the current report that Semiramis had effected her escape from India with about twenty men and Cyrus with about seven, was ambitious, though aware of the difficulties and dangers of the enterprise, to conduct his large army through the same country in safety and triumphantly. In addition to the want of provisions, the scorching heat and the depth of the sand and its burning heat were hard to bear. In some places, too, there were high ridges of sand, so that, besides the difficulty of lifting the legs as out of a deep hole, there were ascents and descents. It was necessary also, on account of the watering places, to make long marches of 200, 400, and even at times of 600 stadia, and generally by night. The camp was pitched at a distance from the wells, and frequently 30 stadia away from them, to prevent the soldiers from drinking to excess from thirst; for many of them threw themselves into the water in their armour, drank of it, and sank below the surface till life was extinct, when their bodies became swollen, and corrupted the shallow waters of the cisterns. Others exhausted by thirst lay exposed to the sun in the middle of the road. Their legs and arms twitched convulsively, and they died like persons seized with cold and shivering. Some turned aside from the road to indulge in sleep, overcome with drowsiness and fatigue. Being thus left behind, some of them lost their way and perished from utter destitution and the heat, while others escaped with their lives after direful sufferings. A winter torrent again, which burst upon them in the night time, destroyed many lives and a great quantity of baggage, besides sweeping away a considerable portion of the royal equipage. The guides through ignorance deviated so far into the interior that the sea was no longer in view."

Arrian has described the misery of Alexander's army through the Gedrosian desert in the following words [38]:

"The soldiers destroyed many of the beasts of burden of their own accord. For when their provisions ran short they came together and killed most of the horses and mules. They ate the flesh of these animals, which they professed had died of thirst and perished from the heat. No one cared to look very narrowly into the exact nature of what was doing, both because of the prevailing distress and also because all were alike implicated in the same offence. Alexander himself was not unaware of what was going on, but he saw that the remedy for the existing state of things was to pretend ignorance of it rather than permit it as a matter that lay within his cognizance. It was therefore no longer easy to convey the soldiers labouring under sickness, nor others who had fallen behind on the march from exhaustion. This arose not only from the want of beasts of burden, but also because the men themselves took to destroying the waggons when they could no longer drag them forward owing to the deepness of the sand. They had done this even in the early stages of the march, because for the sake of the waggons they had to go not by the shortest roads, but those easiest for carriages. Thus some were left behind on the road from sickness, others from fatigue or the effects of the heat or intolerable thirst, while there were none who could take them forward or remain to tend them in their sickness. For the army marched on apace, and in the anxiety for its safety as a whole the care of individuals was of necessity disregarded. As they generally made their marches by night, some of the men were

> *overcome by sleep on the way, but on awaking afterwards those who still had some strength left followed close on the track of the army, and a few out of many saved their lives by overtaking it. The majority perished in the sand like shipwrecked men at sea."*

According to Plutarch, Alexander lost more than three fourths of his army on the way back from India [39]:

> *"He himself, returning by land with the army, marched through the country of the Oreitai, where he was reduced to the sorest straits from the scarcity of provisions, and lost such numbers of men that he hardly brought back from India the fourth part of his military force, though he entered it with 120,000 foot and 15,000 horse. Many perished from malignant distempers, wretched food, and scorching heat, but most from sheer hunger, for their march lay through an uncultivated region, inhabited only by some miserable savages, the owners of a small and inferior breed of sheep, accustomed to feed on sea-fish, which gave to their flesh a rank and disagreeable flavour."*

No military commander would willingly let this happen to his army. That Alexander, who is considered to be the greatest military commander till his time and probably even till our time by many, would let this happen to his army is inconceivable. The only sensible explanation for this turn of events is his defeat at the hands of Porus.

1.7.12 Alexander's historians are liars

The arguments presented so far clearly point to the possibility that Greek historians have lied regarding the outcome of the battle of the Hydaspes. They have turned Alexander's defeat into a fictitious tale of his magnanimity. In fact, one of their own, Strabo (II.I.9) has accused Greek writers of being liars [40]:

> *"Generally speaking, the men who hitherto have written on the affairs of India, were a set of liars. Deimachus holds the first place*

> *in the list, Megasthenes comes next, while Onesicritus and Nearchus, with others of the same class, manage to stammer out a few words [of truth]."*

McCrindle makes the following remarks about Plutarch [41]:

> *"This seems an almost inexcusable mistake on Plutarch's part -- his conducting Alexander as far as the Ganges! The author of the Periplus made the same egregious blunder. It is possible, however, to put a different construction on the expressions used by Plutarch, and to suppose that he wrote so carelessly that he did not mean what his words seem to imply."*

1.7.13 Alexander fought under Porus beyond Hydaspes

We may be asked how and whether Alexander continued his campaign further before deciding to return if he had indeed lost to Porus. Greek writers claim that Alexander subdued a number of kingdoms after his victory over Porus and Porus helped him as a subordinate during these campaigns [42]. The explanation is simple. It was Alexander who fought under the command of Porus, who used this opportunity to expand his territory further. Alexander had to fight with part of his army, while the rest of his army was busy cutting trees and building a fleet for their return journey. This is affirmed by what happened after the campaigns, according to Arrian [43]:

> *"He then assembled the companions and all the ambassadors of the Indians who had come to him, and in their presence appointed Poros king of all the Indian territories already subjugated - seven nations in all, containing more than 2000 cities."*

Why would Porus be made the king of all Indian territories? Greek writers have lied about the result of the battle of the Hydaspes, but they could not conceal the real outcome of the battle, which was the enlargement of the territories ruled by Porus. Now that we have presented arguments in the favor of Porus winning the battle of the

Hydaspes, it is up to the historians to decide what to believe: a series of extraordinary events or a likely set of events consistent with Alexander's character. A warrior of indomitable courage named Porus, who fought fearlessly to save his kingdom from being plundered by Alexander's army, deserves his respectful place in the annals of history. Should he be denied justice and honor just because he didn't employ historians to write the saga of his bravery?

In the following chapters we will consider what transpired after Alexander left India. In order to do that, we will have to take a critical look at how Indians kept track of time.

Notes:

1. McCrindle (1893): 8-9.
2. McCrindle (1893): 9-15.
3. McCrindle (1893): 387.
4. McCrindle (1893): 58-59.
5. McCrindle (1893): 83.
6. McCrindle (1893): 92.
7. McCrindle (1893): 201-202.
8. McCrindle (1893): 273.
9. McCrindle (1893): 202-204.
10. McCrindle (1893): 94-99.
11. McCrindle (1893): 307-309.
12. http://in.rbth.com/blogs/2013/05/27/marshal_zhukov_on_alexanders_failed_india_invasion_25383.html.
13. McCrindle (1893): 109.
14. Anson (2013): 79.
15. Chinnock (1884): 232.
16. McCrindle (1893): 37-38.
17. Chinnock (1884): 217.

18. McCrindle (1893): 269-270.
19. McCrindle (1893): 271.
20. Anson (2013): 124.
21. McCrindle (1893): 26-27.
22. McCrindle (1893): 310.
23. McCrindle (1893): 107-108.
24. McCrindle (1893): 92.
25. McCrindle (1893): 204.
26. McCrindle (1893): 307.
27. McCrindle (1893): 108-109.
28. McCrindle (1893): 231.
29. McCrindle (1893): 112.
30. McCrindle (1893): 284.
31. McCrindle (1893): 212.
32. McCrindle (1893): 212.
33. McCrindle (1893): 110-111.
34. McCrindle (1901): 35-36.
35. McCrindle (1893): 233-234.
36. McCrindle (1893): 234-235.
37. McCrindle (1901): 83-85.
38. McCrindle (1893): 174.
39. McCrindle (1893): 316.
40. Hamilton (1892): 108-109.
41. McCrindle (1893): 310, footnote.
42. McCrindle (1893): 279-282.
43. McCrindle (1893): 133.

"Time heals all wounds, unless you pick at them."
- Shaun Alexander

2. FOOTPRINTS ON THE SANDS OF TIME

It is not the aim of this chapter to give comprehensive details of all the eras prevalent in ancient India. The aim is to present a critical discussion of the eras, which have a bearing on the reconstruction of the part of Indian history covered in this book and in the previous volume, "India before Alexander: A New Chronology". The eras under consideration are discussed below in the chronological order of their respective starting dates.

2.1 Sṛṣṭi (Creation) Era

Sṛṣṭi Saṃvat or creation era was a well established system described in religious as well as astronomical texts such as Manu Smṛti (1.63-73), Sūrya Siddhānta (1.15-20) and Brahmasphuṭasiddhānta (1.26-27). To get a proper perspective, we need to start with the life of Brahmā, the creator God. His lifespan is 100 years, bur those years are different from human years. A year of Brahmā consists of 360 days of Brahmā, which is again different from human days. A day of Brahmā (excluding night) is equal to one Kalpa. It is the calculation of the number of human years in the present Kalpa that has been of significance to Indian astronomers and has a bearing on the discussion to follow in this chapter. One Kalpa has 1000 Mahāyugas (Great ages), also called Chaturyugas (Four ages). Each Mahāyuga has four ages named

Kṛta Yuga (also called Satayuga or Satya Yuga), Tretā Yuga, Dwāpara Yuga and Kali Yuga.

Kali Yuga has 1200 divine years and each divine year has 360 human years, therefore Kali Yuga has 432,000 years. Dwāpara is twice as long as Kali Yuga and has 864,000 years. Tretā Yuga is thrice as long as Kali Yuga and has 1,296,000 years. Kṛta Yuga is four times as long as Kali Yuga and has 1,728,000 years. Beginning and end of each Yuga has Sandhi or junction periods, but these periods are already included in the time shown above and should not be counted separately. Kṛta Yuga has a junction period of 400 divine years or 144,000 human years each in the beginning and at the end. Tretā Yuga has a junction period of 300 divine years or 108,000 human years each in the beginning and at the end. Dwāpara Yuga has a junction period of 200 divine years or 72,000 human years each in the beginning and at the end. Kali Yuga has a junction period of 100 divine years or 36,000 human years each in the beginning and at the end. The sum total of human years in a Mahāyuga or Chaturyuga is simply ten times the age of Kali Yuga, which is 4.32 million human years. As a Kalpa has 1000 Mahāyugas, it is 4.32 billion years long.

One Kalpa is equal to a day of Brahmā, and two Kalpas are equal to a day and night (called Ahorātra in Sanskrit) of Brahmā, which is 8.64 billion years. Thirty Ahorātras of Brahmā is equal to 1 month of Brahmā, which equals 259.2 billion years. Twelve months of Brahmā equal a year of Brahmā, which is 3.1104 trillion years. One hundred years of Brahmā is equal to the life of Brahmā, which is equal to 311.04 trillion years. Now this is a huge number, but this is not the age of our universe. It is the sum total of all the universes that will be created in succession, one after another. The universe is created at the beginning of the day of Brahmā, and destroyed at the end of it. The age of the universe, according to this belief system, is one Kalpa or 4.32 billion years, comparable to ~14 billion years estimated by modern cosmologists.

I have presented above the overall scheme of things in Hindu astronomy. The matter of interest to the Indian astronomers was the time elapsed since the beginning of the present Kalpa. This involves another way of dividing the Kalpa. Each Kalpa has 14 Manvantaras and 15 Sandhis or junctions (13 between the Manvantaras, one in the beginning and one at the end). In this calculation, the junction periods are to be added to the span of Manvantaras to arrive to the total. Each Manvantara has 71 Mahāyugas and each Sandhi equals one Krita age. So the Manvantara is 306.72 million years long and each Sandhi is 1.728 million years long. The total of 14 Manvantaras and 15 Sandhis comes out to 4.32 billion years, same as calculated before. This gives us confidence that we have got the concepts and calculations right.

According to Hindu scriptures and astronomers, we are in the 51st year of Brahmā and in the first Kalpa of this year of Brahmā. We are in the seventh Manvantara now, in which 27 Mahāyugas have passed. We are in the 28th Mahāyuga in which the first three ages have passed. We are in the worst of ages, Kaliyuga, the age of degradation.

With the information we have, let's now proceed to calculate the time passed since the beginning of the present Kalpa. Six Manvantaras and seven junction periods, equivalent to 428.8 Mahāyugas or 1.852416 billion years have passed up to the start of the current Manvantara. The 27 Mahāyugas in the current Manvantara have passed, and thus before the start of the current Mahāyuga, an equivalent of 455.8 Mahāyuga or 1.969056 billion years have passed in this Kalpa. We are in the Kali Yuga of the current Mahāyuga, and thus before the start of the current Kali Yuga, an equivalent of 456.7 Mahāyugas or 1,972,944,000 years have passed since the beginning of the present Kalpa.

It took Brahmā 47,400 divine years or 17.064 million years to create the universe. Subtracting this from the time calculated above, the year of creation era at the beginning of the present Kali Yuga was 1,955,880,000 years. In the year 2015 CE, 5116 years have passed in the Kali age, and thus the current year (2015 CE) in the creation era (Sṛṣti Samvat) is the year 1,955,885,116.

2.2 Saptarṣi Era

The Saptarṣi era has been described by Cunningham in the following words [1]:

> *"The Lok-Kāl, or "common era," called also the Sapt-Ṛṣi-Kāl, or "era of the Seven Ṛṣis," is a cycle of 2700 years divided into twenty seven centenary periods, a new reckoning being started at the beginning of each century. The theory of the cycle is, that the Seven Ṛṣis, or stars of Ursa Major, remain for one century in each of the twenty-seven Nakṣatras, or lunar mansions. All authorities agree in making Aświnī the first of the Nakṣatras, and in stating that the Mahābhārata took place when the Ṛṣis were in the lunar constellation Maghā, the tenth of the series. The Purāṇas, and the practice of all the people who still use this cycle, excepting only the Kaśmiris, agree in making the era of Yudhiṣṭhira the same as the Kali-Yuga. All, however, agree in stating that, at the time of the Mahabharata, the Seven Ṛṣis had already passed 75 years in Maghā. ..."*

How do we know the direction of the movement of the seven sages? We have the following quote from Cunningham in this regard [2]:

> *"Each whole period of 2700 years is called a Chakra, or cycle, in which the Seven Riṣis pass through the 27 Nakṣatras from Aswini to Revati."*

So the direction is forward (Maghā to Pūrva-Phālgunī to Uttara-Phālgunī) according to Cunningham. This is the view held by modern scholars [3]. However, in matters of such great importance for reconstruction of the history of India, we can't go by colonial era wisdom, which is predisposed to supporting the chronology invented by colonial era historians. We need to know the views of the people who were maintaining the ancient records. Fortunately, we have one such reference [4]:

> *"The Hindus have thought proper to connect their chronology with an astronomical period of a most strange nature. It is that of the seven Rishis, or seven stars of the wain, which are supposed to go through the Zodiac, in a reterograde motion in the space of 2700 years. They are at present in the Lunar mansion of "Swāticā" according to the most famous astrologers of Banares, who cautioned me against the erroneous opinion of other astronomers, in various parts of India, who insist that they are now in Anurādhā."*

Based on this information, I have calculated that the direction of motion was assumed to be backward (Maghā to Āśleṣā to Puṣya) by ancient Indians. Now we have enough information to reconstruct the ancient Saptarṣi calendar, which is shown in Figure 2.1 for cycle two and Figure 2.2 for cycle three. The dates for cycles two to four are listed in Table 2.1. As there was no 0 CE and 1 BCE was followed by 1 CE, the starting point of the Saptarṣi era in the first millennium was 25 CE and not 24 CE. We note from Table 2.1 that sages were in Swāti Nakṣatra between 1725 and 1825 CE. According to the astrologers of Benares, sages were in Swāti nakṣatra in 1809 CE, when the above mentioned paper was published. Thus, our calculations are confirmed and the assumption of backward motion (Maghā to Āśleṣā to Puṣya) of sages is verified as opposed to the forward motion (Maghā to Pūrva-Phālgunī to Uttara-Phālgunī) assumed by modern historians and astronomers.

There is a reason for starting the calendar from Mūla nakṣatra in Table 2.1. The reason is based on the following information by Cunningham [5]:

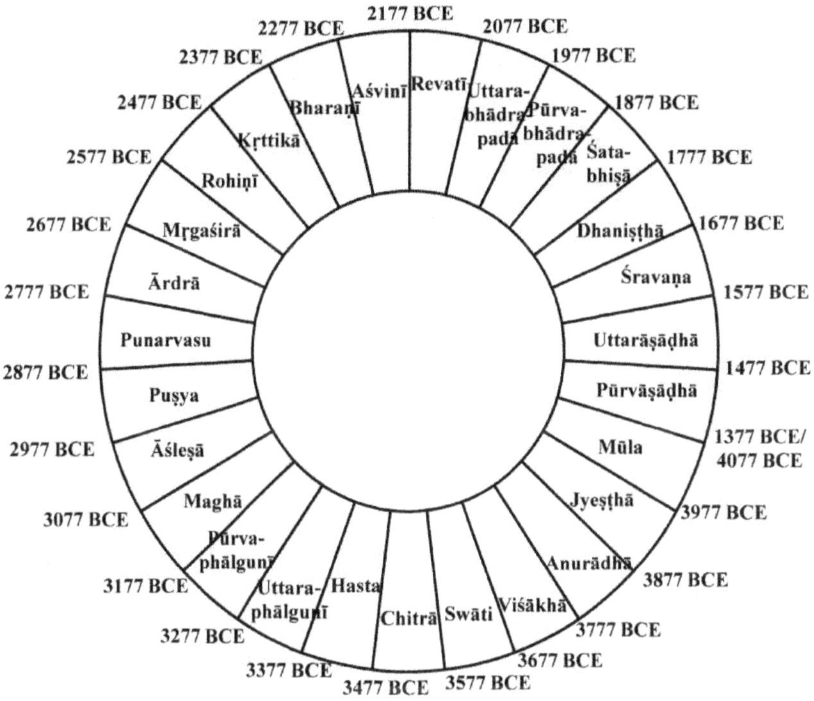

Figure 2.1: Traditional Saptarṣi calendar (Cycle 2)

"On referring to the accounts of ancient India handed down to us by Alexander's companions, I find a curious statement which seems to bear directly on this question of the starting point of Indian chronology. The statement is preserved by Pliny, Solinus, and Arrian. The first says, "Colliguntur ā Libero Patre ad Alexandrum Magnum reges corum CLIV, annis sex millia CCCCLI adjiciunt et menses tres,"-that is, "they reckon from Bacchus to Alexander the Great 154 kings, who reigned for 6451 years and 3 months." As Alexander entered the Panjab in 326 B.C., and left it towards the end of the same year, this account fixes the starting point of Indian chronology to the year $6451^{1/4} + 326 = 6777$ *B.C.*

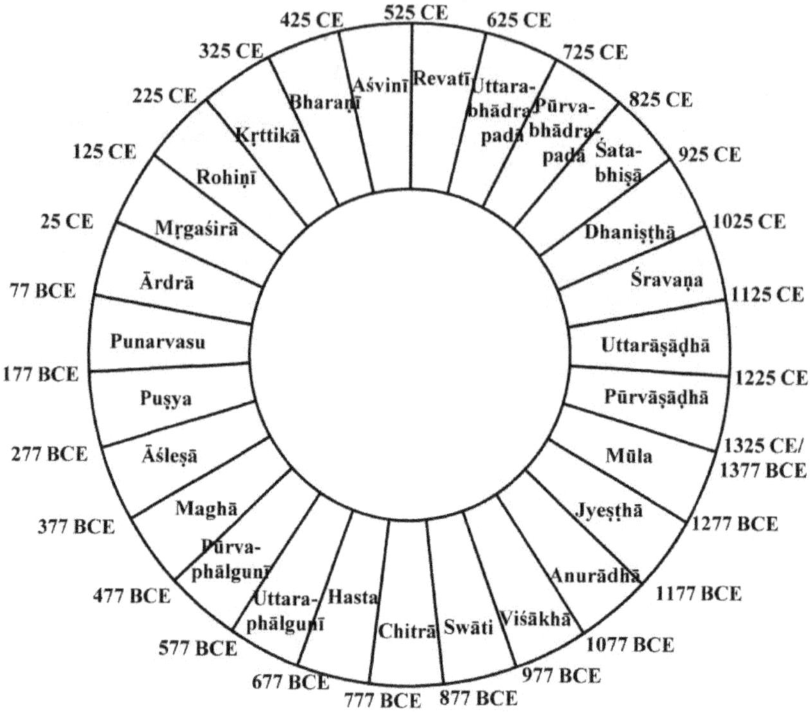

Figure 2.2: Traditional Saptarṣi calendar (Cycle 3)

Now it is a curious coincidence that if another Saptarṣi Chakra of 2700 years be added to 4077 B.C., or the beginning of the Chakra indicated by Vriddha Garga, the initial year will fall in 6777, the very year which was said by the Indians of Alexander's time to be the initial point of their history. This coincidence is certainly very remarkable, and as it is the result of the addition of such a large period as 2700 years, it would seem to point to the conclusion that so early as the time of Alexander, the Saptarṣi Chakra of 2700 years was the common mode of Indian reckoning."

Table 2.1: Saptarṣi calendar

Nakṣatra	**Cycle 2**	**Cycle 3**	**Cycle 4**
Mūla	4077-3977 BCE	1377-1277 BCE	1325-1425 CE
Jyeṣṭhā	3977-3877 BCE	1277-1177 BCE	1425-1525 CE
Anurādhā	3877-3777 BCE	1177-1077 BCE	1525-1625 CE
Viśākhā	3777-3677 BCE	1077-977 BCE	1625-1725 CE
Swāti	3677-3577 BCE	977-877 BCE	**1725-1825 CE**
Chitrā	3577-3477 BCE	877-777 BCE	1825-1925 CE
Hasta	3477-3377 BCE	777-677 BCE	1925-2025 CE
Uttara-Phālgunī	3377-3277 BCE	677-577 BCE	
Pūrva-Phālgunī	3277-3177 BCE	577-477 BCE	
Maghā	3177-3077 BCE	477-377 BCE	
Āśleṣā	3077-2977 BCE	377-277 BCE	
Puṣya	2977-2877 BCE	277-177 BCE	
Punarvasu	2877-2777 BCE	177-77 BCE	
Ārdrā	2777-2677 BCE	77 BCE-25 CE	
Mṛgaśirā	2677-2577 BCE	25-125 CE	
Rohiṇī	2577-2477 BCE	125-225 CE	
Kṛttikā	2477-2377 BCE	225-325 CE	
Bharaṇī	2377-2277 BCE	325-425 CE	
Aśvinī	2277-2177 BCE	425-525 CE	
Revatī	2177-2077 BCE	525-625 CE	
Uttara-Bhādrapadā	2077-1977 BCE	625-725 CE	
Pūrva-Bhādrapadā	1977-1877 BCE	725-825 CE	
Śatabhiṣā	1877-1777 BCE	825-925 CE	
Dhaniṣṭhā	1777-1677 BCE	925-1025 CE	
Śravaṇa	1677-1577 BCE	1025-1125 CE	
Uttarāṣāḍhā	1577-1477 BCE	1125-1225 CE	
Pūrvāṣāḍhā	1477-1377 BCE	1225-1325 CE	

As the Seven Sages were assumed to be in the Maghā asterism during Mahābhārata war (3102 BCE), we can conclude that the sages were in Maghā from 3177-3077 BCE. Knowing that the sages moved clockwise as shown in Figures 2.1 and 2.2 after staying in each asterism for 100 years, we can count backward to determine that the sages were in Mūla nakṣatra from 4077-3977 BCE, which was the beginning of the cycle according to sage Vṛddha Garga. The reason we have labeled the Saptarṣi Cycle starting in 4077 BCE as Cycle 2 is also explained above by Cunningham. The first Saptarṣi cycle started in 6777 BCE with sages being in the Mūla nakṣatra. It is only befitting that the name of the nakṣatra from which the Saptarṣi cycle started is called Mūla, which means root or origin.

So far we have focussed on the calendrical aspect of the Saptarṣi era. It is now time to discuss the scientific basis or the lack of it for the Saptarṣi era. Let's start with a quote by Cunningham again [6]:

> *"Thus Suka, addressing Parikṣit, says: "Of the Seven Riṣis, two are first perceived rising in the sky; and the asterism, which is observed to be at night, even with the middle of those two stars, is that with which the Riṣis are united, and they remain so during a hundred years of men. In your time, and at this moment, they are situated in Maghā. ... The astronomers have been much puzzled to account for the alleged centennial motion of the Seven Riṣis from One Nakṣatra to another, which they admit is not visible to the human race. Thus the commentator Sridhara Swami explains, that 'the two stars which rise first are Pulaha and Kratu; and whichever asterism is in a line south from the middle of those stars is that with which the Seven Riṣis are united, and they so remain for one hundred years." Other explanations are cited by Colebrooke, who closes his account with the opinion of Kamalakara, who observes, that "no such motion of the stars is perceptible. Remarking, however, that the authority of the Puranas and Sanhitas, which affirm their*

revolution, is incontrovertible, he reconciles faith and experience by saying, that the stars themselves are fixed; but the Seven Ṛṣis are invisible deities, who perform the stated revolution in the period specified." "

Here is the statement of the problem: we have a calendrical system of 2700-year-cycle based on the assumed motion of seven sages with the sages residing in each nakṣatra for exactly 100 years. However, the sages take nearly 26,000 years for a complete revolution around the pole. This phenomenon is known as the precession of the equinoxes. These two facts are hard to reconcile. The best explanation to my knowledge is provided by Sule et al. as follows [7]. As each nakṣatra is of a different spatial span based on the stars in the constellation, the actual time taken by the sages is different for each nakṣatra. Also, the apparent motion of the sages has not been uniform over the ages. During the period 2200-2100 BCE, the sages took about a hundred years to traverse the Puṣya nakṣatra based on the brightest stars in this small nakṣatra. This information was later generalized due to misinterpretation, and formed the basis of the Saptarṣi calendar.

Regardless of its faulty scientific basis, a proper understanding of the Saptarṣi calendar as a simple counting method is invaluable in developing the proper chronology of ancient Indian history.

2.3 Bhārata War Era

According to the Aihole inscription of Pulikeśin II, when 3735 years had passed since the Bhārata war, 556 years of Śaka kings had also passed. As the 556 Śālivāhana Śaka is equivalent to 634 CE, 3735 years before that date gives us 3102 BCE as the year of the Bhārata war.

However, this is not the exact year of the Bhārata war, but the date of the start of the Kali age. To be specific, the Bhārata or Mahābhārata war took place 36 years before the start of the Kali age. So, the Bhārata war was believed to have taken place in 3138 BCE. The timing of the Bhārata war and the start of the Kali age were used interchangeably in ancient India and most of the times both refer to the era starting in 3102 BCE.

2.4 Kali Era

The start of Kali era in 3102 BCE is well established. We have the following quotes from Cunningham regarding the Kali era:

> *"The Kali-Yuga, or fourth age of Hindu Chronology, dates from the year 3102 B.C.; the year 1, expired or completed, being B. C. 3101." [8]*

> *"So universal is the belief that the date of the Kali-Yuga is the same as that of the Mahābhārata, that the native almanacs state it as a positive fact. Thus Professor Bhandarkar quotes the following from an ordinary Hindu Panchāṅga of Bombay: 'In the Kali-age there are six founders of eras. First, there was Yudhiṣṭhira in Indraprastha, whose era lasted for 3044 years. The second was Vikrama at Ujayani, whose era had a run of 135 years. The third was Śālivāhana at Pratiṣṭhāna.' Here the era of Yudhiṣṭhira is made the same as that of the Kali-Yuga, which also dates from 3044 years before the era of Vikrama." [9]*

After the invasion of Alexander, the idea of conjunction of planets in 3102 BCE was picked up by the Greeks, but they associated this event with a deluge instead of the Bhārata war. The idea then passed on to Persians and subsequently to Muslims. Here is what Abul Fazl says about the era of the deluge [10]:

> *"The era of the deluge: This era is computed from this event; the year is natural, solar, the month natural, lunar. The year begins from the entry of the Sun into Aries. Abu Māshar of Balkh based his calculations regarding the mean places of the starts on this era from which to the present year 4,696 years have elapsed."*

Abul Fazl started writing the Akbarnāmā in 1589 CE after receiving official sanction from Akbar. Āin-I-Akbari is the third volume of Akbarnāmā and consists of five books. Abul Fazl was assassinated in 1602 CE, so Āin-I-Akbari was written sometime in the 1590s. As he calculated that it was 4,696 years since the deluge, it is not hard to see that the start of the era is 3102 BCE – the same as that of the Kali era. The quote above, from Abul Fazl can be dated to 1594 CE.

We have positive confirmation of the date of the Kali era and the era of the deluge being identical from a paper by Prof. B.L. van der Waerden, the Dutch mathematician and historian of mathematics [11]:

> *"... Persian astronomical tables, the so-called Tables of the Shāh, which were composed under Khusro Anūshīrvān about 560 A.D. and revised under Yazdigerd III about 640 A.D., were also based on the assumption of a conjunction of all planets near 0° Aries in 3102 B.C. The methods of computation of these Tables were closely related to the Hindu methods, ... In all texts based on Persian sources, a Deluge is supposed to begin at the moment of the conjunction."*

The credit for calculating the date of conjunction as February, 3102 BCE is given to Greeks by Prof. B.L. van der Waerden [11]. However, this is highly doubtful. We show in Section 2.8 below that this calculation was done by Jain astronomers in the 8th century BCE or before, a date that takes us to the very beginning of Greek civilization.

2.5 Yudhiṣṭhira Era

Technically, the Yudhiṣṭhira era starts from the day when king Yudhiṣṭhira reached heaven, which was 25 years after the start of the Kali era. However, we need to keep in mind that the Bhārata war, Kali and Yudhiṣṭhira eras have been used interchangeably in ancient India. Most of the times, the starting date of 3102 BCE is presumed for all three eras. Sometimes, a distinction could be made and 3138 BCE could be assigned for the Bhārata war, 3102 BCE for the start of the Kali era and 3077 BCE for the start of the Yudhiṣṭhira era. We should also notice that the starting points of the Saptarṣi era and the Yudhiṣṭhira era are the same in terms of dropped centuries. So, the whole idea of the Saptarṣi staying in the Maghā asterism for 25 years longer after the start of the Kali era was to devise an unforgettable link between the Kali era and the Saptarṣi era and synchronize the Yudhiṣṭhira era with the Saptarṣi era. What strikes us most about this exercise is the passion of our extremely intellectual ancestors in making sure that their legacy would be passed on from generation to generation to their descendants.

2.6 Erroneous Saptarṣi Era

An erroneous version of the Saptarṣi era was started by Kalhaṇa, a Brāhmaṇa from Kashmir, who lived in the 12th century CE. He misinterpreted a verse written by Varāhamihira and opined that the time of Yudhiṣṭhira was 653 years after the beginning of the Kali era. This is proven by the following statement by Cunningham [12]:

> *"The Purāṇas, and the practice of all the people who still use this cycle, excepting only the Kashmiris, agree in making the era of Yudhishthira the same as the Kali-Yuga."*

Modern historians have instead accused Varāhamihira of creating this misunderstanding. Let me quote Cunningham again [13]:

> *"All, however, agree in stating that, at the time of the Mahabharata, the Seven Riṣis had already passed 75 years in Maghā. But as Varāha places the Great War 653 years after the beginning of the Kali-Yuga, or in 2449 B.C., that year should have been the 76th of the tenth Nakṣatra, and the 976th year of the*

> *cycle. This would fix the first year of each centenary period to the 25th year of each century B.C., and to the 76th year of each century A.D. But to prevent the confusion that would thus have arisen, Varāha simply ignored the generally accepted belief that the Ṛiṣis had spent 75 years in Maghā when the Mahabharata took place and retained the initial points of the Saptarṣi centuries - only bringing Maghā down from B.C. 3177 (or 3102 + 75) to B.C. 2477."*

Let us ignore what Cunningham is crediting to Varāhamihira, because the mistake was made by Kalhaṇa and not Varāhamihira. This passage suggests that the beginning of the Saptarṣi era in terms of dropped centuries remained the same even for Kalhaṇa's miscalculations. Even though Kalhaṇa separated the beginning of the Kali era from the demise of Yudhiṣṭhira by 653 years, he actually shifted the cycle of the Saptarṣis by 700 years. In effect, Kalhaṇa shifted the entrance of the Saptarṣis in Maghā asterism from the accepted date of 3177 BCE to 2477 BCE. Since the beginning of the Saptarṣi era in terms of dropped centuries remained the same, it is expected that the first year of each century for erroneous Saptarṣi calendar of Kalhaṇa corresponded with the 25th year of each century of the Common Era. This was indeed the case as shown below [14]:

> *"Now this last is the same name that is used by Kalhaṇa Pandit of Kashmir, who says: ...*
>
> *'The 24th year of the Laukika corresponds with the year 1070 of the Saka-Kal.'*
>
> *From this statement we learn that the year 1 of the Laukika coincided with 1047 of the Saka, or A.D. 1125; and as the cycle was a centenary one, the first year of each century must have corresponded with the 25th year of each Christian century."*

Based on the information presented above, we can modify the ancient Saptarṣi calendar to show the erroneous Saptarṣi calendar of Kalhaṇa. Starting from 2477 BCE as discussed above, the erroneous Saptarṣi calendar of Kalhaṇa is shown in Figure 2.3 for cycle one and Figure 2.4 for cycle two. The dates for cycles one and two are listed in Table 2.2.

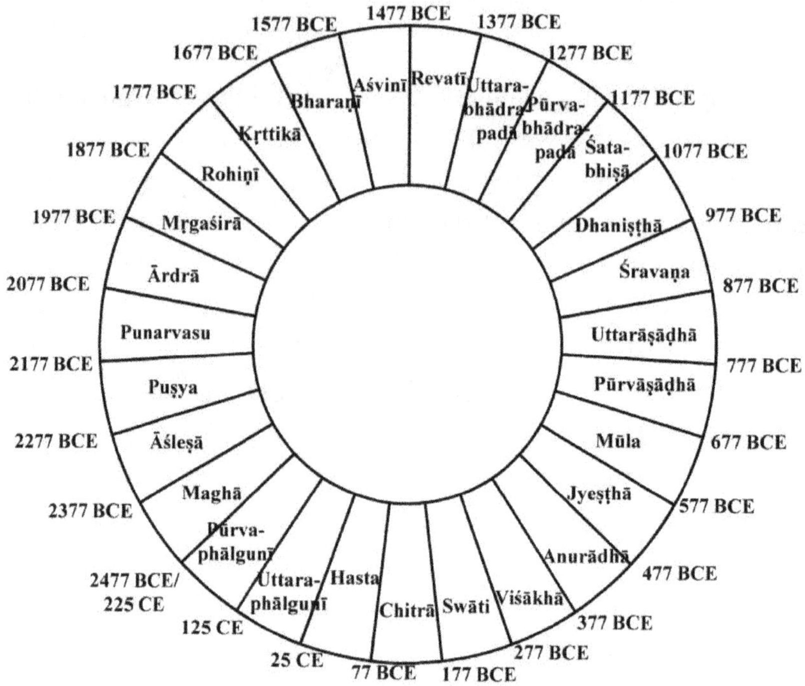

Figure 2.3: Erroneous Saptarṣi calendar (Cycle 1)
based on Kalhaṇa's misinterpretation

So what else was the difference then between the Sapatarṣi era of Kaśmir compared to the Sapatarṣi era of the rest of India apart from a difference of seven centuries in the start date of the Sapatarṣi cycle? It seems that the other difference was the starting month of the era as described below:

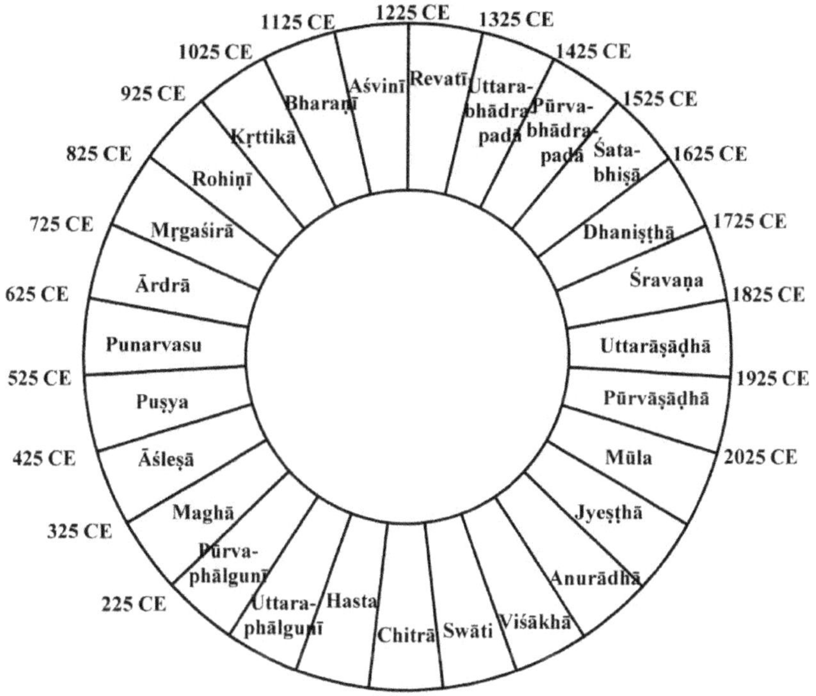

Figure 2.4: Erroneous Saptarṣi calendar (Cycle 2)
-- based on Kalhaṇa's misinterpretation

"The reckoning of the Lok-Kal, as now used in Kaśmir and the other hill states, is by the common luni-solar years beginning on Chaitrasudi 1, or the new moon of Chaitra. The cycle consists of 27 centuries, each counting from 1 to 100 years, when a new reckoning is begun. The first year of each century corresponds with the 25th year of each Christian century. According to Abu Rihan the people of Multan had only recently adopted the Kaśmiri reckoning from Chaitra, while in Sindh and Kanauj they still reckoned the year from Mankhir (that is from Margasiras or Agrahayana)." [15]

Table 2.2: Erroneous Saptarṣi calendar
based on Kalhaṇa's misinterpretation

Nakṣatra	Cycle 1	Cycle 2
Maghā	2477-2377 BCE	225-325 CE
Āśleṣā	2377-2277 BCE	325-425 CE
Puṣya	2277-2177 BCE	425-525 CE
Punarvasu	2177-2077 BCE	525-625 CE
Ārdrā	2077-1977 BCE	625-725 CE
Mṛgaśirā	1977-1877 BCE	725-825 CE
Rohiṇī	1877-1777 BCE	825-925 CE
Kṛttikā	1777-1677 BCE	925-1025 CE
Bharaṇī	1677-1577 BCE	1025-1125 CE
Aśvinī	1577-1477 BCE	1125-1225 CE
Revatī	1477-1377 BCE	1225-1325 CE
Uttara-Bhādrapadā	1377-1277 BCE	1325-1425 CE
Pūrva-Bhādrapadā	1277-1177 BCE	1425-1525 CE
Śatabhiṣā	1177-1077 BCE	1525-1625 CE
Dhaniṣṭhā	1077-977 BCE	1625-1725 CE
Śravaṇa	977-877 BCE	1725-1825 CE
Uttarāṣāḍhā	877-777 BCE	1825-1925 CE
Pūrvāṣāḍhā	777-677 BCE	1925-2025 CE
Mūla	677-577 BCE	
Jyeṣṭhā	577-477 BCE	
Anurādhā	477-377 BCE	
Viśākhā	377-277 BCE	
Swāti	277-177 BCE	
Chitrā	177-77 BCE	
Hasta	77 BCE-25 CE	
Uttara-Phālgunī	25-125 CE	
Pūrva-Phālgunī	125-225 CE	

2.7 Nanda Era

According to our interpretation of a verse from the Sumatitantra [16], the Nanda era started 2000 years after the Kali era. This implies that the Nanda era started in 1102 BCE. Details of our interpretation and discussion of the relationship of the Nanda era with other ancient Indian eras are presented in Section 2.10 below under the heading "Imperial Gupta Era". Reference to King Nanda has been made in the inscription of King Khāravela. This makes perfect sense as both the Nandas and the Khāravela were Jains. Modern history books say that a canal was extended to the capital by Khāravela 103 or 300 years after Nanda. However, this may be based on a wrong interpretation of the Hathigumbha inscription. According to Sten Konow, a canal was built 103 or 300 years after King Nanda, which was extended to the capital by Khāravela [17]. It cannot be inferred from the inscription as to which King Nanda the inscription refers to. Reference to Nanda has no bearing on the dating of Khāravela, whose date must be determined by other information provided in his inscription, such as the kings he encountered during his military expeditions.

2.8 Kṛta/Mālava Era

Modern Indian historians declare that the Vikrama era was earlier known as the Kṛta era or the Mālava era and all three have the starting date of 57 BCE [18]. Though there is evidence of the Kṛta and Mālava eras being equivalent, there is no evidence for these two eras to be equivalent to the Vikrama era. This distinction is of critical interest to followers of Indian history, as on this distinction rests the historicity of the most endearing monarch of ancient India, Emperor Vikramāditya, immortalized in the legends of Vikrama and Vetāla.

Many historians hold the view that the Mālava era was instituted by the Mālava tribe, which had a republican system of governance. The reason for this hypothesis is the use of the word *gaṇa* with Mālava. However, this view is erroneous as the term *gaṇa* has been used to mean a method of calculation and not as a system of governance. Vyāsa explains this as follows [19]:

> *"Rock inscriptions found in Mandasaur made during fifth and sixth centuries call the era "Mālavānām Gaṇasthityā". However, they are made by kings ruling Mālavā such as Naravarmana, Kumāragupta, Bandhuvarmana and Prabhākara. Thus Gaṇa here does not mean a system of governance by Gaṇa, but way of counting as in Gaṇanā."*

Some other historians have tried to associate the Mālava era with the tribe of Mallas, whom Greek historians have named Malloi, and described as neighbours of Oxydrakai (Kṣudraka). This theory is baseless as the Mallas and Kṣudrakas were at the northwestern boundaries of India during the invasion of Alexander in 4th century BCE, while Ujjain, the capital city of the ancient Malwa, is so old that traditionally it has been known as "Anādi Ujjayinī", the city without a beginning in time.

Two inscriptions from the time of Kumāragupta-I are extremely important in narrowing down the beginning of the Mālava era. Both inscriptions were written on a Sun temple in Mandsaur city in the Malwa region of Madhya Pradesh. In ancient times, this city was known as Daśapura. The first inscription was written when the temple was constructed, and the second inscription was written when the temple was repaired. The dates of both inscriptions are given in the Mālava era instead of the Gupta era. This makes it even more interesting. These two inscriptions are reproduced below for further discussion [20]:

> *"Perfection has been attained! May that Sun protect you, who is worshipped by the hosts of the gods for the sake of existence, and by the Siddhas who wish for supernatural powers, (and) by ascetics, entirely given over to abstract meditation (and) having worldly attractions well under control, who wish for the final liberation of the soul, and, with devotion, by saints, practising strict penances, (who wish to become) able to counteract curses; (and) who is the cause of the destruction and the commencing (again) of the universe! Reverence to that Sun, whom (even) the Brāhmanical sages, though*

they knew the knowledge of the truth (and) exerted themselves, failed to comprehend; and who nourishes the whole of the three worlds with (his) rays diffused in all directions; who, when he is risen, is praised by Gandharvas, gods, Siddhas, Kinnaras, and Naras; and who grants (their) desires to those who worship (him)! May that Sun, decorated with glorious beams, protect you, - who shines, day after day, with the mass of (his) rays flowing down over the wide and lofty summit of the lordly mountain of dawn, (and) who is of a dark-red colour like the cheeks of intoxicated women!

(Line 3.) - From the district of Lāṭa, which is pleasing with choice trees that are bowed down by the weight of (their) flowers, and with temples and assembly-halls of the gods, and with vihāras, (and) the mountains of which are covered over with vegetation, to (this) city of Daśapura there came, full of respect,-first, in thought; and afterwards (in person) in a band, together; with (their) children and kinsmen, - men who were renowned in the world for (skill in their) craft (of silk-weaving), and who, being manifestly attracted by the virtues of the kings of the country, gave no thought to the continuous discomforts produced by the journey and its accompaniments. And in course (of time) this (city) became the forehead-decoration of the earth, which is adorned with a thousand mountains whose rocks are besprinkled with the drops of rut that trickle down from the sides of the temples of rutting elephants, (and) which has for (its) decorative ear-ornaments the trees weighed down with flowers. Here the lakes, crowded with kārandava-ducks, are beautiful,-having the waters close to (their) shores made variegated with the many flowers that fall down from the trees growing on the banks, (and) being adorned with full-blown waterlilies. The lakes are beautiful (in some places); with the swans that are encaged in the pollen that falls from the waterlilies shaken by the tremulous waves; and in other places with the waterlilies bent down by the great burden of their filaments. Here the woods are adorned with lordly trees, that are bowed down by the weight of their flowers and are full of the sounds of the flights of bees that

hum loudly through intoxication (caused by the juices of the flowers that they suck), and with the women from the city who are perpetually singing. Here the houses have waving flags, (and) are full of tender women, (and) are very white (and) extremely lofty, resembling the peaks of white clouds lit up with forked lightning. And other long buildings on the roofs of the houses, with arbours in them, are beautiful,-being like the lofty summits of (the mountain) Kailāśa; being vocal with songs (like those) of the Gandharvas; having pictured representations arranged (in them); (and) being adorned with groves of waving plantain trees. Here, cleaving asunder the earth, there rise up houses which are decorated with successions of storeys; which are like rows of aerial chariots; (and) which are as pure as the rays of the full-moon. This (city) is beautiful (through) being embraced by two charming rivers, with tremulous waves, as if it were the body of (the god) Smara (embraced) in secrecy by (his wives) Prīti and Rati, possessed of (heaving) breasts. Like the sky with the brilliant multitudes of planets, it shines with Brāhmaṇs endowed with truth, patience, self-control, tranquillity, religious vows, purity, fortitude, private study, good conduct, refinement, and steadfastness, (and) abounding in learning and penances, and free from the excitement of surprise.

(L. 8.) - So assembling together, (and) day by day received into greater friendship by (their) constant associates, (and) honourably treated like sons by the kings, in joy and happiness they settled in (this) city. Some of them (became) excessively well acquainted with the science of archery, (in which the twanging of the bow is) pleasing to the ear; others, devoting themselves to hundreds of excellent achievements, (became) acquainted with wonderful tales; and others, unassuming in (their) modesty (and) devoted to discourses of the true religion, (became) able to say much that was free from harshness (and yet was) salutary. Some excelled in their own business (of silk-weaving); and by others possessed of high aims, the science of astrology was mastered; and even to-day others of them, valorous in battle, effect by force the destruction of (their)

enemies. So also others, wise, possessed of charming wives, (and) belonging to a famous and mighty lineage, are decorated with achievements that befit (their) birth; and others, true to (their) promises (and) firm in friendship with the accompaniment of confidence, are skilled in conferring favours upon (their) intimates. (And so) the guild shines gloriously all around, through those who are of this sort, and through others who, overcoming the attachment for worldly objects; being characterised by piety; (and) possessing most abundant goodness, - (are) very gods in an earthly habitation.

(L. 11.) - (Just as) a woman, though endowed with youth and beauty (and) adorned with the arrangement of golden necklaces and betel-leaves and flowers, goes not to meet (her) lover in a secret place, until she has put on a pair of coloured silken cloths,-(so) the whole of this region of the earth, is (almost superfluously) adorned through them, (as if) with a silken garment, agreeable to the touch, variegated with the arrangement of different colours, (and) pleasing to the eye.

(L. 12) - Having reflected that the world is very unsteady, being blown about by the wind life the charming ear-ornaments, (made of) sprigs, of the women of the Vidyādharas (and similarly) the estate of man; and also accumulations of wealth large (though they may be),- they became possessed of a virtuous (and) stable understanding and then;-

(L. 13.) - While Kumāragupta was reigning over the (whole) earth, whose pendulous marriage-string is the verge of the four oceans; whose large breasts are (the mountains) Sumeru and Kailāsa; (and) whose laughter is the full-blown flowers showered forth from the borders of the woods;-

(L. 13.) - There was a ruler, king Viśvavarman, who was equal in intellect to Śukra and Brihaspati, who became the most eminent of princes on the earth; (and) whose deeds in war were equal to (those of) Pārtha; - who was very compassionate to the unhappy; who fulfilled his promises to the miserable and the distressed; who was

excessively full of tenderness; (and) who was a very tree of plenty to (his) friends, and the giver of security to the frightened, and the friend of (his) country;-

(L. 14.) - His son (was) king Bandhuvarman, possessed of firmness and statesmanship; beloved by (his) kinsmen; the relative, as it were, of (his) subjects; the remover of the afflictions of (his) connections; pre-eminently skilful in destroying the ranks of (his) proud enemies. Handsome, youthful, dexterous in war, and endowed with humility, king though he was, yet was he never carried away by passion, astonishment and other (evil sentiments); being the very incarnation of erotic passion, he resembled in beauty, even though he was not adorned with ornaments, a second (Kāmadeva) armed with the bow that is made of flowers. Even today, when the long-eyed lovely women of (his) enemies, pained with the fierce pangs of widowhood, think of him, they stagger about through fear, in such a way as to fatigue (their) firm and compact breasts.

(L. 16.) - While he, the noble Bandhuvarman, the best of kings, the strong-shouldered one, was governing this city of Daśapura, which had been brought to a state of great prosperity, a noble (and) unequalled temple of the bright-rayed (Sun), was caused to be built by the silk-cloth weavers, as a guild, with the stores of wealth acquired by (the exercise of their) craft;-(a temple) which, having broad and lofty spires, (and) resembling a mountain, (and) white as the mass of the rays of the risen moon, shines, charming to the eye, having the similarity of (being) the lovely crest-jewel, fixed (in its proper place), of (this) city of the west.

(L. 17.) - In that season which unites men with (their) lovely mistresses; which is agreeable with the warmth of the fire of the rays of the sun (shining) in the glens; in which the fishes lie low down in the water; which (on account of the cold) is destitute of the enjoyment of the beams of the moon, and (sitting in the open air on) the flat roofs of houses, and sandal-wood perfumes, and palm leaf-fans, and necklaces;-in which the waterlilies are bitten by the frost;

which is charming with the humming of the bees that are made happy by the juice of the full-blown flowers of the rodhra and priyamgu-plants and the jasmine-creepers; in which the lavalī -trees and the solitary branches of the nagaṇā-bushes are made to dance with the force of the wind that is harsh and cold with particles of frost; - (and) in which (the cold induced by) the falling of frost and snow is derided by the close embraces of the large and beautiful and plump and bulky breasts and thighs of young men and (their) mistresses, completely under the influence of love;-when, by (the reckoning from) the tribal constitution of the Mālavas, four centuries of years, increased by ninety-three, had elapsed; in that season when the low thunder of the muttering of clouds is to be welcomed (as indicating the approach of warmth again); - on the excellent thirteenth day of the bright fortnight of the month Sahasya, this temple was established, with the ceremony of auspicious benediction.

(L. 19.) - And, in the course of a long time, under other kings, part of this temple fell into disrepair; so now, in order to increase their own fame, the whole of this most noble house of the Sun has been repaired again by the munificent corporation; - (this temple) which is very lofty (and) pure; which touches the sky, as it were, with (its) charming spires; (and) which is the resting-place of the spotless rays of the moon and the sun at (their) times of rising. Thus, when five centuries of years, increased by twenty, and nine years had elapsed; on the charming second lunar day of the bright fortnight of the month Tapasya;-in the season when (Kāmadeva), whose body was destroyed by Hara, develops (his number of five) arrows by attaining unity with the fresh bursting-forth of the flowers of the aśoka and ketaka and sinduvāra-trees, and the pendulous atimuktaka-creeper, and the wild-jasmine;-when the solitary large branches of the nagaṇā-bushes are full of the songs of the bees that are delighted by drinking the nectar; (and) when the beautiful and luxuriant rodhra-trees swing to and fro with the fresh bursting forth of (their) flowers, - the whole of this noble city was decorated with (this) best

> *of temples; just as the pure sky is decorated with the moon, and the breast of (the god) Śārngin with the kaustubha-jewel. As long as (the god) Īśa wears a mass of tawny matted locks, undulating with the spotless rays of the moon (on his forehead); and (as long as) (the god) Śārngin (carries) a garland of lovely waterlilies on his shoulder;-so long may this noble temple endure for ever!*
>
> *(L. 23.) - By the command of the guild, and from devotion, (this) temple of the Sun was caused to be built; and this (eulogy) that precedes was, with particular care, composed by Vatsabhatti. Hail to the composer and the writer, and those who read or listen (to it)! Let there be success!"*

Before we continue with the discussion of the Mālava era based on these crucial inscriptions, let us just point out that this inscription refers to the month Sahasya, when the Sun temple was constructed, and month Tapasya, when the Sun temple was repaired. These months are solar months, similar to the months January to December, but have lost their popularity to lunar months. These solar months were related to the six seasons as follows:

Vasanta (spring)	-	Madhu-Mādhava
Grīṣma (summer)	-	Śukra-Śuchi
Varṣā (rainy season)	-	Nabha-Nabhasya
Śarada (autumn)	-	Īśa-Urja
Hemanta (cool season)	-	Saha-Sahasya
Śiśira (winter)	-	Tapa-Tapasya

Returning to the discussion of the Mālava era, the first Mandsaur inscription mentions that Kumāragupta (I) was ruling the world when a Sun temple was built by the guild of silk weavers in the Mālava year 493. The inscription was continued in Mālava year 529, when the temple was repaired by the guild of silk weavers. Since the Imperial Guptas were contemporaries of Seleucus and other Greek kings in the alternative chronology, the Mālava era should begin sometime in the late eighth century BCE. The dates of 725 BCE and 711 BCE have been proposed, as shown below:

> *"They arbitrarily brought Malwa Gana era from 725 B.C. to 57 B.C., and dared proclaim that this was identical with the Vikrama Era or Azes Era." [21]*

> *"Counting from 315 B.C. as the accession-date of Chandragupta I, we get for the years 95-135 of Kumāragupta I the reign-period 220-180 B.C. ... Then, to reach the starting-point of the Mālava Era, we may count either 493 years backward from 218 B.C. or 529 from 182 B.C. We arrive at 711 B.C." [22]*

The problem is that these two dates seem to be arbitrary and no justification is given as to why the Mālava/Kṛta era has a starting point of 725 BCE or 711 BCE. To proceed further, and to find out the actual starting date of the Mālava/Kṛta era, we will need to turn our attention to the genius of Jain astronomers. We will start with the following quotation from Al-Biruni about the astronomer Āryabhaṭa [23].

> *"I have not been able to find anything of the books of Āryabhaṭa. All I know of him I know through the quotations from him given by Brahmagupta. The latter says in a treatise called Critical Research on the Basis of the Canons that according to Āryabhaṭa the sum of the days of a caturyuga is 1,377,917,500, i.e. 300 days less than according to Pulisa. Therefore Āryabhaṭa would give to a kalpa 1,590,540,840,000 days. According to Āryabhaṭa and Pulisa, the kalpa and caturyuga begin with midnight which follows after the day the beginning of which is the beginning of the kalpa, according to Brahmagupta. Āryabhaṭa of Kusumapura, who belongs to the school of the elder Āryabhaṭa, says in a small book of his on Al-ntf (?), that "1008 caturyugas are one day of Brahman. The first half of 504 caturyugas is called utsarpini, during which the sun is ascending, and the second half is called avasarpini, during which the sun is descending. The midst of this period is called sama, i.e.*

equality, for it is the midst of the day, and the two ends are called durtama (?)." "

We take notice here that according to Al-Biruni, Āryabhaṭa divides the timespan of Caturyuga in Utsarpini, Avasarpini, Sama, and Durtama. Al-Biruni has made his comments based on verse 9 in the Kālakriyā chapter (reckoning of time) of the celebrated Āryabhaṭīya written by Āryabhaṭa. What is so special about that? These are divisions of time in various ages according to the Jain system of knowledge. In addition, Āryabhaṭa says in Āryabhaṭīya that he was born 23 years before (or after according to alternative interpretations) 60 times 60 years of the Kali era had passed. Saying 60 times 60 instead of 3600 is further evidence of Āryabhaṭa-I being a Jain, as the number 60 is an important number in Jain astronomy. In fact, Āryabhaṭa had combined Hindu and Jain systems of reckoning, and he has come in for some criticism from Brahmagupta on this account.

According to Āryabhaṭa, before the start of the current Kali yuga, 1,986,120,000 years had passed [24], which is drastically different from that given by Brahmagupta as 1,972,944,000 years [25]. The number given by Brahmagupta is the same as that calculated in section 2.1, and so this is congruent with the accepted belief system of Hindus. Āryabhaṭa and Brahmagupta lived less than two centuries apart, and we may wonder how Āryabhaṭa came up with a number that is more than 13 million years apart from the traditionally accepted value. It was so because he adopted a simplified model. Āryabhaṭa says in verse 3 of the Daśagītikā (ten introductory verses) of the Āryabhaṭīya that there are 14 Manus in a kalpa with each manu having 72 yugas. It further says that 6 manus, 27 yugas and 3 yugapadas had passed in this kalpa. Further in the chapter Kālakriyā (reckoning of time), verse 8 of the Āryabhaṭīya, Āryabhaṭa says that a yuga consists of 12,000 years of the gods and 1,008 yugas make a day of Brahmā. We now have enough information to calculate the time elapsed since the beginning of the kalpa according to Āryabhaṭa. Each yuga is 4,320,000 years as a year of gods has 360 human years. Each manvantara, or age of Manu, has 72 yugas, which is 311,040,000 years. Each yugapāda equals one fourth of a yuga and has 1,080,000 years. When we add up the time for 6 manus, 27 yugas and 3 padas, we get 1,986,120,000 years. What we find is that Āryabhaṭa had developed a much simpler system than that described in Section 2.1, having done away with junction periods between Manvantaras and dividing a Mahāyuga or Chaturyuga in four equal parts instead of the traditional division in the ratios 4:3:2:1. He then integrated this system with the Jain system by dividing a Kalpa in Utsarpiṇī (acending) and Avasarpiṇī (descending). According to Āryabhaṭīya [26], the first half of a kalpa is called Utsarpiṇī (acending) and the second half is called Avasarpiṇī (descending). The beginning and end points are called Duṣṣamā, and the middle point is called Suṣamā. The point we are making here by going into these details is that the Jain and Hindu astronomers worked very closely together, and throughout history the relationship between Jains and Hindus has been symbiotic, with both sustaining each other. In fact, going a step further, I would say that Hindu astronomers borrowed liberally from Jain astronomers and that the Mālava era has its origin in Jain astronomy and cosmology. Let us try to explore this further using the following quote [27]:

> *"The Yuga system mentioned by Āryabhaṭa (probably a Jain who speaks about Jain Yuga system of Suṣmā-Duṣmā etc. divisions within each Yuga) begins in BC 3102, and is composed of 4800 years. Since he divides the Yuga into four equal parts, one Yugapada would be 1200 years. Three Yugapada will mean 3600 years."*

It is fascinating to know that Jains also had a cyclical time system, which had its starting point in 3102 BCE. This also happens to be the starting point of the Kali Yuga in Hindu astronomy. Clearly, one is borrowed from the other, and we are inclined to say that it was the Hindu astronomers who borrowed the calculations made by the Jain astronomers. More corroborative evidence is presented in the next chapter, where we propose that the origin of the legends of Vikramāditya can be traced to Jain astronomers.

The next critical piece of information for the present discussion is that a popular version of the Jain time cycle had exactly 4800 years. We want to point out that the above quote is an explanation of the famous verse by Āryabhaṭa in which he describes the time of his birth [28]. The three Yugapadas could also mean the past three yugas in the current Chaturyuga. Therefore, we need corroborative evidence in support of the hypothesis, which we present in section 2.10 on the Imperial Gupta era. Sreenadh, in an article titled "Āryabhaṭa and Jain Yuga system" has given a detailed breakdown of the timeline of Jain Yugas based on the starting point of 3102 BCE and 4800 years time cycle as follows [29]:

1. Utsarpiṇī (3102 BCE to 702 BCE)
   i. Duṣṣamā Duṣṣamā (3102 BCE to 2702 BCE)
   ii. Duṣṣamā (2702 BCE to 2302 BCE)
   iii. Duṣṣamā Suṣamā (2302 BCE to 1902 BCE)
   iv. Suṣamā Duṣṣamā (1902 BCE to 1502 BCE)
   v. Suṣamā (1502 BCE to 1102 BCE)
   vi. Suṣamā Suṣamā (1102 BCE to 702 BCE)
2. Avasarpiṇī (702 BCE to 1698 CE)
   i. Suṣamā Suṣamā (702 BCE to 302 BCE)
   ii. Suṣamā (302 BCE to 98 CE)
   iii. Suṣamā Duṣṣamā (98 CE to 498 CE)
   iv. Duṣṣamā Suṣamā (498 CE to 898 CE)
   v. Duṣṣamā (898 CE to 1298 CE)
   vi. Duṣṣamā Duṣṣamā (1298 CE to 1698 CE)

In the Jain time cycle, Suṣamā denotes happiness and Duṣṣamā denotes unhappiness. Suṣamā Suṣamā denotes extreme happiness and Duṣṣamā Duṣṣamā denotes extreme unhappiness. The Jain time cycle starts with a period of extreme unhappiness and gradually moves to a period of extreme happiness in the first half. In the second half, it starts with a period of extreme happiness and ends with a period of extreme unhappiness. We note that Avasarpiṇī, the second half of Jain time cycle, started in 702 BCE with a period of extreme happiness. We propose that this is the beginning of the Mālava era. The era was started by Jain astronomers at Ujjain, which was the most important centre of ancient Indian astronomy. Ujjain was established as an eminent centre of astronomy due to its location on the Tropic of Cancer. As Hindu astronomers borrowed Jain concepts and assimilated them in the Hindu belief systems, the boundaries between the two systems started to blur. With the passage of time, as Hindu beliefs became popular with the masses, the period of extreme happiness was identified with Kṛta age, the age when good qualities are at the height, and the Mālava era came to be known as the Kṛta era. As Samudragupta and Chandragupta II took the title of Vikramāditya, which was based on the Jain tradition of the legendary ruler of Ujjayinī in Malwa region, it is obvious that the Gupta rulers took pride in using the Mālava era. This is the reason Mālava era has been used during the time of Kumāragupta-I.

As both the Mālava era and the Vikrama era have Jain origins, Jain authors later got confused between these eras. They had the memory of an era starting 470 years after the passing away of Lord Mahāvīra. In light of the new chronology developed in this book, Lord Mahāvīra's death needs to be counted from the Mālava era instead of the Vikrama era. Accordingly, the year of Lord Mahāvīra's death, based on our calculation and reasoning, is 1172 BCE. As he had lived for 72 years, he lived between 1244-1172 BCE.

2.9 Cyrus Śaka Era

The Cyrus Śaka era was introduced in India by Varāhamihira, whose forefathers came to India in the wake of Alexander's invasion of Persia. It is named after the Persian king -- Cyrus the Great. The era was instituted to celebrate the founding of the Achaemenid Empire of Persia. The starting date of the Cyrus Śaka era is 550 BCE. We have presented a detailed discussion of this era in "India before Alexander: A New Chronology" [30]. Confusion of the Cyrus Śaka era with the Śālivāhana Śaka era is the cause of major inaccuracies in Indian history. Also, the association of Śaka with an era by Varāhamihira later gave rise to another meaning to the word Śaka, that of an era itself. Thus, later on the words Śaka and Samvat became synonymous. This is why all Indian calendars contained the name of Śakakārakas or the creators of eras (Śaka), which were listed as six, three in the past and three in the future.

2.10 Imperial Gupta era

The alternative chronology being developed in this book has the Imperial Guptas as contemporaries of the Greek kings, starting with Alexander the Great. This implies that the Imperial Gupta era should have a starting point towards the end of the 4th century BCE instead of the currently accepted starting date of 319 CE. We will start the discussion of the Imperial Gupta era with the evidence of the Gokak plates, which prove the existence of a Gupta era a few centuries before the start of the Christian era.

The Gokak copper plates were discovered in 1926 from a house in Gokak in the then Belgaum district of the Bombay Presidency, and its details were published by N. Lakshminarayana Rao in Epigraphia Indica [31]. The importance of these plates comes from the mention of an "Aguptāyika era" that has historians in a bind. Aguptāyika means related to Guptas. The relevant passage from the grant is reproduced below [31]:

> *"When forty five after eight hundred of the years of the Aguptayika kings in (i.e. belonging to) this ever flowing and prosperous spiritual lineage of the wise Varddhamana, the twenty fourth of the Tirthankaras, had elapsed, the illustrious adhiraja Indrananda, the*

son of Vijayananda-Maddhyamaraja, the bright son who had risen in the firmament of the illustrious and pure Sendraka family and who was the favourite of the illustrious Dejja-Maharaja, born of the Rashtrakuta dynasty, gave, in order to increase the merit of his ancestors as well as of himself, land measuring fifty nivartanas by the royal measure in the village of Jalara situated near the mountain in the division of Kashmandi to Aryyanandyacharya who belonged to the Jambukhanda-gana and was well versed in sacred knowledge, systems of philosophy and penance, for offering worship incessantly to the idol of the divine Arhat, for the (maintenance of) teachers, the sick and the old and for the service of ascetics."

Rao makes the following comments about the Gokak plates in his paper [31]:

"The grant registered in the charter was made when 845 years of the Aguptayika kings had expired. This date is specially noteworthy for we do not know anything of the Aguptayika kings with whom it is connected. This is the first inscription known to us making mention of these kings. No details about them are, however, recorded in this document except that they belonged to the spiritual lineage of Varddhmana, the 24th Jain Tirthankara. The name of the era started by these personages namely the Aguptayikas or the reckoning to which it belonged are questions which can be decided only by future researches. Paleographically the document may be ascribed to about the 6th or 7th century of the Christian era. No reckoning is known at present which would give for 845 an equivalent in the sixth or seventh century of that era. If however, we follow the Jain tradition and place the commencement of the reign of the Maurya emperor Chandragupta in B.C. 312-13 – for this appears to be the correct date of his accession – and consider it to be the starting point of the Aguptayika era we get A.D. 532-33 as the date of our record."

Noted historian D.C. Sircar makes the following comments about the Aguptayika era [32]:

> *"Aguptayika era may be roughly assigned to 845-645 = 200 B.C. … But we can scarcely accept the evidence of a single inscription regarding the existence of a genuine era starting from about 200 B.C. in the face of the overwhelming negative evidence.… The story may have been fabricated by the astronomer at Dejja-Maharaja's court."*

We should note the propensity to declare anything that does not fit the accepted chronology as fabrication. We might as well ask what the possible motive was for the astronomer at Dejja-Maharaja's court to fabricate the story. It is logical to assume that the details of the grant were engraved as believed at that time. Professor Richard Saloman also put the beginning of the era referred in the Gokak plates to the third or second century BCE [33].

Our next bit of evidence comes from a text called the Sumati Tantra, which is the first book on astronomy from Nepal. A copy of the Sumati Tantra is available in the British Museum. From the original verses in Sanskrit quoted by Malla [34], we can extract the following information:

> *Yudhiṣṭhira and Duryodhana were present at the junction of Kali (with Dwapara). Both of them continued for 2000 years, Nanda ruled for 800 years, Chandragupta for 132 years, Śūdraka for 247 years, Śaka king for 498 years and Mānadeva for 304 years.*

Malla [34] says it is not clear whether these figures refer to the duration of the rule of a king, or of the dynasty, or of the use of the epoch year. If the duration of a king's reign was specified, then it is a case of pious fabrication.

Malla quotes many researchers who have tried to make sense of these verses, but no one has succeeded, and the easiest way out is to deem the whole thing a fabrication. This approach is obvious from the title of the article itself, which is "Mānadeva Samvat: An Investigation into a Historical Fraud." Malla also quotes noted historian K.P. Jayaswal to have given the following opinion [34]:

"It is clear that the author of the chronology took chief reigns as landmarks, and not always eras. There were Yudhiṣṭhira Era, Nanda and Śaka Eras, but there was no Chandragupta Era, there was no Sudraka Era. There is no trace of an Era of Manadeva I."

These historians are mistaken, because prima facie, this medieval text is about the six eras -- the Yudhiṣṭhira, Nanda, Chandragupta, Śudraka, Śaka, and Mānadeva eras. It gives the date of its composition as 3981 years (sum of 2000+800+132+247+498+304 years) since the start of the Kali age, which sums up to 879 CE. How can anyone deny the existence of the Chandragupta, Śudraka and Mānadeva eras, when it is so clearly written in a text that is more than a millennium old? If only the historians had tried to make sense out of these seemingly obscure verses instead of belittling them and declaring them as forgery, they would have discovered that these verses shake the very foundation of modern Indian history. So, let's try to understand what these verses are indicating.

In fact, it is quite obvious what these verses indicate. Obviously, they are not defining the ruling period of kings as no one lives for 2000 years. They are not defining how long the individual eras lasted, as the use of Śaka era is still continuing. What they are defining simply is the period between the specified eras. So, these verses give the following very important information:

The Nanda era started 2000 years after the Kali era. The Chandragupta era started 800 years after the Nanda era. The Śūdraka era started 132 years after the Chandragupta era. The Śaka era started 247 years after the Śūdraka era. The Mānadeva era started 498 years after the Śaka era. The Sumatitantra was written in the 304th year of the Mānadeva era.

As the Kali era started in 3102 BCE, according to these verses, the Nanda era started in 1102 BCE, the Chandragupta era started in 302 BCE, the Śudraka era started in 170 BCE, the Śaka era started in 78 CE, the Mānadeva era started in 576 CE, and the text Sumatitantra was written in 880 CE. As there was no zero BCE or zero CE and 1 CE followed 1 BCE, 247 years from 170 BCE falls in 78 CE instead of 77 CE. We should note that the starting date of the well-known Śālivāhana Śaka era is 78 CE, and this calculation exactly matches with it. This provides a solid confirmation for our own interpretation.

Let us now turn our attention to determine the date of the Buddha based on the information of the Nanda era just derived. We are going to use the information from the Purāṇas for this purpose as given by Pargiter [35].

> *"Ajātaśatru will be king 25 years. Darśaka will be king 25 years. After him Udāyin will be king 33 years. That king will make as his capital on the earth Kusumpura on the south bank of the Ganges in his fourth year. Nandivardhana will be king 40 years. Mahānandin will be 43 years. … As son of Mahanandin by a śudra woman will be born a king, Mahapadma (Nanda), who will exterminate all kṣatriyas. Thereafter kings will be of Śudra origin. Mahapadma will be sole monarch, bringing all under his sole away. He will be 88 years on the earth. He will uproot all kṣatriyas, being urged on by prospective fortune. He will have 8 sons, of whom Sukalpa will be the first; and they will be kings in succession to Mahapadma for 12 years. A Brahman Kautilya will uproot them all; and, after they have enjoyed the earth 100 years, it will pass to the Mauryas."*

We now need to decide whether the starting point of the Nanda era corresponds to the reign of Nandivardhana, Mahānandin, or Mahāpadma Nanda. To make the proper choice, we take note that Mahāvīra and Buddha were contemporaries. We had determined earlier in Section 2.8 that Mahāvīra lived between 1244-1172 BCE. To be consistent with these dates, the Nanda era needs to start with the beginning of the reign of Nandivardhana. Based on this assumption, Table 2.3 shows the chronology of Magadha kings.

Table 2.3: The chronology of Magadha kings

King	**Reign in years**	**Proposed Chronology**
Ajātaśatru	25	1185-1160 BCE
Darśaka	25	1160-1135 BCE
Udāyin	33	1135-1102 BCE
Nandivardhana	40	1102-1062 BCE
Mahānandin	43	1062-1019 BCE
Mahāpadma Nanda	88	1019-931 BCE
Eight Nandas	12	931-919 BCE

The Buddha died sometime during the reign of Ajātaśatru, because we are told that Ajātaśatru had asked for a part of the remains of the Buddha and built a Buddhist temple/stupa over the remains. According to current history books, the Buddha died in the eighth year of Ajātaśatru's reign [36]. Thus, the Parinirvāṇa of the Buddha took place in 1178 BCE, based on information from Table 2.3 above. As the Buddha had lived for 80 years, we can calculate that he lived between 1258-1178 BCE. These dates fit very well with the date of Lord Mahāvīra (1244-1172 BCE), determined earlier. Since these dates have been arrived at from two completely independent considerations, evidence of Sumatitantra for Lord Buddha and connecting the Mālava era with the death of Lord Mahāvīra, we get confidence in these dates and the reasoning used to arrive at these dates. We should also note that we have arrived at the dates of Lord Buddha and Chandragupta I of the Imperial Gupta dynasty based on the evidence of Sumatitantra, a text from Nepala. While Lord Buddha was born in present day Nepala, Chandragupta-I married a Lichchhavi princess and Lichchhavis had moved to Nepala subsequent to the rise of the Imperial Guptas. It should come as no surprise that the correct dates for both Lord

Buddha and Chandragupta-I has come from a source close to their native places rather than from the far away land of Śrī Laṅkā.

Let us now return to the discussion of the Gupta era. It is obvious that the Chandragupta era of 302 BCE specified in Sumatitantra refers to Chandragupta-I of the Imperial Guptas and not to Chandragupta Maurya, because it places the start of the Nanda era in 1102 BCE and the Mauryas followed soon after the Nandas. However, we have another start date of the Imperial Gupta era, according to Al-Biruni [37]:

> *"As regards the Guptakala, people say that the Guptas were wicked powerful people, and that when they ceased to exist this date was used as the epoch of an era. It seems that Valabha was the last of them, because the epoch of the era of the Guptas falls, like that of the Valabha era, 241 years later than the Śakakala."*

As detailed in Section 2.9, the Cyrus Śaka era started in 550 BCE and subtracting 241 years from that, we get 309 BCE as the starting date of the Imperial Gupta era. As the date of 302 BCE based on Sumatitantra involves round numbers (2000 years from Kali, then 800 years from Nanda), we expect the date to be approximate, not exact. So, how do we pinpoint the accurate starting date of the Imperial Gupta era? Is it 309 BCE or a few years before or after 302 BCE? Fortunately, we have some information that can help in pinpointing the accurate date of the start of the Imperial Gupta era. Professor Harry Falk has presented a set of data from the Imperial Gupta records that have not been satisfactorily explained so far. Each record contains two dates, one in the Imperial Gupta era and the second in an unknown era [38]. Professor Falk interprets the second set of data to be the continuation of the Kuṣāṇa era, where figures representing hundreds have been dropped. Since the Imperial Guptas come before Kuṣāṇas in the chronology we can reject this out of hand. To find an alternative explanation, let us just look at the raw data:

Table 2.4: Some Gupta era dates

Gupta Monarch	Gupta era date	Unknown era date
Chandragupta II	Erased	61
Not mentioned	Not given	70
Kumāragupta	112	5
Kumāragupta	121	15

If we take a start date of 309 BCE for the Imperial Gupta era, years 112 and 121 will correspond to 197 BCE and 188 BCE respectively. If we look at Figure 2.1, we find that the Saptarṣi entered a new asterism in 276 BCE, which will give corresponding years in Saptarṣi cycle as 79 and 88 respectively. This does not match the last column, and so it does not add up. A start date of 302 BCE will give corresponding years in the Saptarṣi cycle as 86 and 95 respectively, which does not work either. What if the last column is from the continuation of the Mālava era that we know was used by the Imperial Guptas from the Mandsaur inscriptions? There are inscriptions from the time of Kumāragupta which use the Mālava era as the system of reckoning. In Section 2.8, we have shown that the Mālava era started in 702 BCE. If an era continues for several centuries, people may start dropping the figures for hundreds. The nearest centennial start of the Mālava era prior to the dates under consideration is 202 BCE, which will give the continuation years as 5 and 14 corresponding to a start date of 309 BCE for Imperial Gupta era. One number matches in the last column, while one other misses by one. This is to be expected anyway, as the Gupta era dates have difference of only nine years, while the dates in the unknown era have a difference of ten years. Such a situation can arise when the starting months of the two eras are not the same. As we have successfully explained, the historical data presented in Table 2.4, we get confidence in the starting dates of 702 BCE for the Mālava era and 309 BCE for the Imperial Gupa era. In fact, we are now in a position to fill the two missing dates in the second column under the Gupta era, and also identify the unknown Gupta monarch in the first column of Table 2.4. The first two dates in the last column obviously refer to the centennial beginning of the Mālava era in 302 BCE. Counting from that, the dates 61 and 70 refer to 241 BCE and 232 BCE respectively. Counting from the beginning of the Gupta era in 309 BCE, these years will refer to 68 and 77 of the Imperial Gupta era respectively. To identify the unnamed Gupta monarch, we will need to create the new Imperial Gupta chronology with the starting date of 309 BCE. This is shown in Table 2.5 below. The data on regnal years has been calculated from the dynastic chart given in the paper "Later Gupta History: Inscriptions, Coins and Historical Ideology" by Michael Willis [39]. The unnamed monarch in Table 2.4, corresponding to the Imperial Gupta era 77, can now be identified as Chandragupta II.

It is now time to revisit the two Mālava era dates mentioned in Section 2.8. With 702 BCE as starting date of Mālava/Kṛta era, the year 493 of Mālava year corresponds to 209 BCE. This is the year when the Sun Temple was constructed and Kumāragupta-I was ruling, according to the Mandsaur inscription. According to Table 2.5 below, Kumāragupta (I) was indeed ruling in 209 BCE. This should give us further confidence in the starting dates of the Mālava/Kṛta and Gupta eras worked out in this chapter.

We now have a consistent framework for developing the new chronology of Indian history. The year 529 of the Mālava year corresponds to 173 BCE, when the Sun Temple of Mandsaur was repaired. The inscription does not mention the ruler at that time when repair was done, presumably because Kumāragupta-I was still ruling or the place was in a state of turmoil, and it was not clear who was ruling or would be ruling soon.

Table 2.5: Chronology of Imperial Gupta Kings

Gupta Monarch	**Regnal years**	**Current Timeline [39]**	**Proposed Timeline**
Chandragupta I	1-31	319-50 CE	309-294 BCE*
Samudragupta	31-57	350-76 CE	294-252 BCE
Chandragupta II	57-96	376-415 CE	252-213 BCE
Kumāragupta I	96-128	415-447 CE	213-173 BCE
Ghatotkachagupta	129-136**	448-455 CE	
Skandagupta	137-148	456-467 CE	172-161 BCE
Narasiṃhagupta	148-155	467-474 CE	161-154 BCE
Kumāragupta II	155-157	474-476 CE	154-152 BCE
Budhagupta	158-169	477-488 CE	151-140 BCE
Vainyagupta II	189	506 CE	120 BCE
Viṣṇugupta	196	515 CE	113 BCE

* Further explanation is provided in Chapter 4.

**Most historians include this period under Kumāragupta I and consider Skandagupta to have directly succeeded Kumāragupta I.

Table 2.5 shows that Ghatotkachagupta was ruling at that time, according to Willis [39], but this is disputable as recorded in the note under Table 2.5. It is more plausible that Kumāragupta-I was still ruling, but this was the final year of his rule. Skandagupta succeeded him in the following year, and it is well known from the Bhitari pillar inscription that Skandagupta had to quell an internal uprising and a deadly invasion by the Hūṇas at the very beginning of his rule. The years of turmoil preceding Skandagupta's rule can now provide the backdrop in which the Sun Temple of Mandsaur fell into despair. Kumāragupta-I was lost in the make-believe world of brainwashed devotees convinced by his missionaries that his messages of peace were being followed in faraway lands of Greece and Egypt, while, in reality, barbarians were pounding at the gates and the empire was crumbling from within.

2.11 Śūdraka Era

The Śūdraka era started in 170 BCE as discussed in Section 2.10. We are now in a position to identify King Śūdraka after whom this era was named. From Table 2.5 above, we can see that the Gupta monarch Skandagupta was King Śūdraka. I have identified Kumāragupta I as Devānāmpriya Priyadarśī in "India before Alexander: A New Chronology" [40]. The messages of peace sent to Greek kings by his father Kumāragupta I as Devānāmpriya Priyadarśī were interpreted as signs of weakness, as has universally happened throughout history, and resulted in an internal rebellion as well as foreign invasions. We know that Skandagupta started his reign by crushing the internal rebellion and repelling the dreaded Hūṇas from India. As the date of the Śūdraka era falls within a couple of years of Skandagupta's coronation, according to Table 2.5, we can confidently say that the Śūdraka era was established to celebrate the crushing defeat of the Hūṇas by Skandagupta, who took the title Vikramāditya for saving India from barbarian invaders. The name Śūdraka may be based on the low origins of Skandagupta [41].

2.12 Vikrama Era

According to Indian tradition, the Vikrama era was instituted to commemorate the death of Emperor Vikramāditya in 57 BCE. Emperor Vikramāditya had extirpated the Śakas and made the whole population free of debt. Cunningham has described the Vikrama era thus [42]:

> *"The Vikramāditya Samvat, or era of Vikramāditya, is reckoned from the vernal equinox of the year 57 BC, and the completion of the Kali-Yuga year 3044. It is used all over Northern India, except in Bengal, where the Śaka era has been generally adopted. It is used also in Telingana and Gujarat; but in the latter province the year does not begin until seven months later than in the north, or with the 1st of Kartik-Sudi, which now falls during October, but which,*

at the beginning of the Christian era, fell between the middle of September and the middle of October."

Modern history has denied the existence of an Emperor Vikramāditya in 57 BCE and given credit to king Azes for instituting this era. In the last chapter of this book, we will identify the real Emperor Vikramāditya, who ruled prior to 57 BCE. Emperor Vikramāditya is the subject of the most endearing legends of ancient India. We will show in the next chapter that the legends of Vikramāditya have their origin in the works of Jain astronomers. Cunningham has made the following remarks regarding the Jain origins of the Vikrama era [43]:

"In the Jain books also there is very early mention of the Vikrama Samvat. Thus the Satrunjaya Mahatmya professes to have been written 477 years after Vikrama, or in AD 420, when 'Siladitya, king of Vallabhi, expelled the Buddhists from Saurașṭra, recovered Satrunjaya and other places of pilgrimage from them, and erected many Jain temples.' The era of Vikrama also is said to have been established by Vikramarka Raja 470 years after Mahavira, or in 527 - 470 = 57 BC. From the way in which he is spoken of as 'honouring the advice of Siddha Sena Suri as the words of Jain,' it would appear that Vikramarka was a Jain, which would account for the use of his era in the Jain books, as well as for the non-mention of it in early Brahmanical inscriptions."

We will take up the detailed discussion of the legends of Vikramāditya in the next chapter.

2.13 Azes Era

For a long time, history books have proclaimed King Azes, a Śaka ruler, as the founder of the Vikrama era. Here is a quote to this effect [44]:

"Azes (Aya in Kharosthi) was another powerful Śaka ruler in the Northwest who initiated a dynastic era beginning in 58/57 B.C.

> *which later became identified with the so-called Vikrama era still used in South Asia."*

However, modern historians cannot explain why an era started by Azes would become known as the Vikrama era. Emperor Vikramāditya's rule extended over most of India, while Azes was a petty king in comparison. According to recent research by Falk and Bennet, the dates of the Azes era are not compatible with a beginning in 57 BCE and the Azes era started somewhere between 48-46 BCE [45]. It had nothing to do with the Vikrama era, which coincides with the death of Emperor Vikramāditya.

2.14 Śālivāhana Śaka Era

The Śālivāhana Śaka era has the starting date of 78 CE. It is described by Cunningham thus [46]:

> *"The reckoning of the Saka era begins with the vernal equinox of the Kali-Yuga year 3179, or A. D. 78. But as the Indians count only by completed years, the year 1 begins with the vernal equinox of Kali Yuga 3180, or A. D. 79. In Northern and Southern India it is usually employed along with the luni-solar calendar; but in Bengal it is generally used with the solar calendar. In converting Saka dates into Christian reckoning, 78 years must be added to the given date; and vice versa to convert Christian dates into Saka reckoning, 78 years must be deducted from the former."*

Just like the Vikrama era, the Śālivāhana Śaka era was also instituted to celebrate the extirpation of Śakas. No wonder, Al-Biruni got confused between the two monarchs credited for these deeds of bravery. Al-Biruni describes the Śaka era in this manner [47]:

> *"The epoch of the era of Śaka or Śakakala falls 135 years later than that of Vikramāditya. The here-mentioned Śaka tyrannised over their country between the river Sindh and the ocean, after he had made Aryavarta in the midst of this realm his dwelling-place. He*

> *interdicted the Hindus from considering and representing themselves as anything but Śakas. Some maintain that he was a Śudra from the city of Almansura; others maintain that he was not a Hindu at all, and that he had come to India from the west. The Hindus had much to suffer from him, till at last they received help from the east, when Vikramāditya marched against him, put him to flight and killed him in the region of Karur, between Multan and the castle of Loni. Now this date became famous, as people rejoiced in the news of the death of the tyrant, and was used as the epoch of an era, especially by the astronomers. They honour the conqueror by adding Śri to his name, so as to say Śri Vikramāditya. Since there is a long interval between the era which is called the era of Vikramāditya and the killing of Śaka, we think that that Vikramāditya from whom the era has got its name is not identical with that one who killed Śaka, but only a namesake of his."*

According to Indian tradition, the Śaka era was instituted by the Śālivāhana king Gautamīputra Śātakarṇi. Modern historians insist that this era was instituted by a foreigner as the name of the era is Śaka. They refuse to acknowledge that Śaka in this case simply means "era" as in the word "Śakakāraka" meaning maker (Kāraka) of an era (Śaka). After the introduction of the Cyrus Śaka era in India by Varāhamihira, the term Śaka gradually came to mean an era in addition to its original meaning of a specific group of foreigners. This understanding is important in correcting the chronology of ancient India. Most Indian inscriptions do not specify the era they are referring to and simply give the year with the word Samvat or Śaka. The inscriptional dates need to be assessed based on the compatibility with other supporting evidence. While performing this assessment, inscriptional dates need to be checked using all feasible eras to get the best fit with all available information.

2.15 Kuṣāṇa Era

For a long time, history books have proclaimed Kuṣāna emperor Kaniṣka as the founder of the Śalivāhana Śaka era, even though Kaniṣka was not a Śaka by any stretch of the imagination. Here is how Smith justifies it [48]:

> *"Opinions differ, but it is probable that the Saka era of A.D. 78 dates from the accession or coronation of Kaniṣka, the Śaka king. Indians authors use the term Śaka vaguely to denote all foreigners from beyond the passes, and would have had no hesitation in calling a Kuṣāna a Saka. In later ages the era was known as that of Salivahana."*

However, this theory has received a death blow after Professor David Pingree published the first survey of the contents of Yavanajātaka written by Sphujidhvaja and said the following [49]:

> *"From this verse it is clear that the Era of the Kuṣānas, (i.e., of Kaniṣka?) is not the same as the Saka Era...."*

Though Professor Pingree didn't find the exact relationship between theŚaka era and the Kuṣāṇa era, Professor Harry Falk found the following after careful analysis [49]:

> *"The elapsed years of the Kuṣanas in combination with 149 (change into) the time of the Śakas."*

Based on this information, the beginning of the Kuṣāṇa era is in 227 CE. However, Professor Falk has proposed the starting date of 127 CE invoking the hypothesis of dropped hundreds. Even though there is no ambiguity in the meaning of the text, the problem is that modern history has placed the Imperial Guptas in the fourth century CE and the Kuṣāṇas and the Imperial Guptas cannot be contemporary as both would be ruling the same territory at the same time. To avoid this improbability, the rule of the Kuṣāṇas has to end before the rule of the Imperial Guptas begins. This makes the starting date of 227 CE for the Kuṣāṇa era untenable in the framework of the currently accepted Indian historical chronology. As the time of the Imperial Guptas in the chronology we are proposing is several centuries before the Kuṣāṇas, there is no such restriction placed on the chronology, and the Kuṣāṇa era can begin in 227 CE as the text of Yavanajātaka proclaims.

2.16 Erroneous Gupta Era/Vallabhī Era

The Imperial Gupta era beginning 309 BCE started 241 years after the Cyrus Śaka era. After many centuries, people became confused between the Cyrus Śaka era and the Śālivāhana Śaka era, and assumed erroneously that the Gupta era started 241 years after the Śālivāhana Śaka era, which fell in 319 CE. This explains the use of the Gupta year 300 in the Ganjam inscription of Śaśānka, who was the contemporary of Harṣavardhana in the seventh century. As by this time, the Imperial Guptas were long gone, Al-Biruni concluded that the start of the Gupta era marks the end of the Imperial Guptas. Based on Al-Biruni's comments, Cunningham describes the start of the Gupta era in the following maner [50]:

> *"The Gupta-Kal, or Gupta era, is not mentioned by any native writer, although it is found in several ancient inscriptions, as well as on the coins of the Gupta kings. It is however noticed by Abu Rihan, who makes the singular mistake of dating it from the epoch of their extermination, and of confounding it with the era of Balabhi. Now the initial point of the Balabhi era is known absolutely from Colonel Tod's inscription, which makes the year 1 = 319 A.D., which is precisely the same date that is assigned to it by Abu Rihan, who says, that it is posterior to Saka by 241 years, or 241 + 78 = 319 A.D. But as he goes on to say 'Apparemment Ballaba suivit immediatement les Guptas,' it is clear that the Guptas must have reigned before A.D. 319. ... For these reasons I much prefer the earlier date of A.D. 167 as the first year of the Gupta era."*

In a strange coincidence, the starting date of both the Gupta era and the Vallabhī era is considered the same by modern historians. The Vallabhī era has the starting point of 319 CE based on an inscription quoted by Tod and as described by Cunningham [51]:

> *"The initial point of the Balabhi-kal, or era of Balabhi, is fixed by the account of Abu Rihan, as well as by the other dates recorded in Tod's inscription, to the year 319 A.D. According to the former, it was 241 years posterior to the Saka, or 78 + 241 = 319 A.D. According to the inscription, Sunday the 13th Aṣadha-Badi of the year 945 of Srimad Balabhi, fell in the year 662 of Muhammad, 1320 of Vikrama, and 151 of the Siva Singha Samvat. The first year of the Balabhi era was fixed by Tod by deducting 975 from 1320, which gives 375 of the Vikrama Samvat as the year 1 of the Balabhi Samvat. Then, deducting 56 from 375, he obtained 319 A.D. as the equivalent in the Christian era."*

It seems that the era starting 319 CE was later termed Vallabhī to avoid confusion with the original Gupta era. Otherwise, it is hard to justify why two eras would have the same starting point.

2.17 Harṣa Era

The Harṣa era was established to commemorate the accession of Harṣa Vikramāditya to the throne in CE 606. Modern history knows of Harṣa Vikramāditya as Harṣa Śīlāditya. Al-Biruni was confused about the existence of another Harṣa era with the starting date of 457 BCE. This confusion is based on the following statement by Al-Biruni [52]:

> *"The Hindus believe regarding Śrī Harṣa that he used to examine the soil in order to see what of hidden treasures was in its interior, as far down as the seventh earth; that, in fact, he found such treasures; and that, in consequence, he could dispense with oppressing his subjects (by taxes, &c.). His era is used in Mathurā and the country of Kanoj. Between Śrī Harṣa and Vikramāditya*

there is an interval of 400 years, as I have been told by some of the inhabitants of that region. However in the Kaśmīrian calendar I have read that Śrī Harṣa was 664 years later than Vikramāditya. In face of this discrepancy I am in perfect uncertainty, which to the present moment has not yet been cleared up by any trustworthy information."

Indian tradition does not know of any great king Harṣa worthy of starting an era 400 years before the Vikramāditya era of 57 BCE. There seems to be a simple solution to this mess, and it relates to Al-Biruni's misunderstanding of what was told to him. He was probably told that the era of Harṣa Vikramāditya started 400 years before his time, which he misunderstood as the Harṣa era started 400 years before the time of Vikramāditya. Al-Biruni came to India around CE 1017, which is roughly 400 years after the accession of Harṣa to the throne. Regarding Harṣa Śilāditya being Harṣa Vikramāditya, we present the following from noted historian D.C. Sircar [53]:

"This suggestion could be supported by the fact that, in Indian tradition, Harṣa Śilāditya was persistently confused with the legendary Śakāri Vikramāditya of Ujjayinī, probably because Harṣa was the founder of an era like the traditional originator of the Vikrama saṃvat."

Harṣa Vikramāditya is considered to have converted to Buddhism. There is no evidence for this conversion based on Indian sources. Harṣa Vikramāditya was a devout Śaiva and his respect for Hiuen Tsang was in keeping with the Hindu tradition of tolerance. It cannot be taken as a proof of conversion. Chinese travellers were experts in telling tall tales, and everything they claim has to be taken with a grain of salt.

With this background of ancient Indian eras, we are now in a position to unravel the mysteries behind one of the most endearing legends of India -- the legends of Vikramāditya.

Notes

1. Cunningham (1883): 11.
2. Cunningham (1883): 12.
3. Sule et al. (2007).
4. Wilford (1809a).
5. Cunningham (1883): 14-15.
6. Cunningham (1883): 9-14.
7. Sule et al. (2007).
8. Cunningham (1883): 31.
9. Cunningham (1883): 13.
10. Jarrett (1891): 22.
11. van der Waerden (1980).
12. Cunningham (1883): 11.
13. Cunningham (1883): 11-12.
14. Cunningham (1883): 6.
15. Cunningham (1883): 15.
16. Malla (2005).
17. Konow, S. (1923).
18. Thapar (2003): xiii.
19. Vyāsa (1990): 30.
20. Fleet (1888): 84-88.
21. Venkatachelam (1953): 30.
22. Sethna (1989): 499.
23. Sachau (1910a): 370-371.
24. Colebrooke (1873): 364.
25. Brahmasphuṭasiddhānta 1.26-27.
26. Āryabhaṭīya, Chapter Kālakriyā, Verse 9.
27. Kumar et al. (2013): 17.
28. Āryabhaṭīya, Chapter Kālakriyā, Verse 10.
29. https://groups.yahoo.com/neo/groups/jainhistory/conversations/messages/801.
30. Roy (2015).
31. Rao (1931-32).

32. Sircar (1965): 326.
33. Saloman (1998): 194.
34. Malla (2005).
35. Pargiter (1913): 69.
36. Majumdar et al. (2001): 37.
37. Sachau (1910b): 7.
38. Falk, H. (2004).
39. Willis (2005).
40. Roy (2015).
41. Willis (2005).
42. Cunningham (1883): 47.
43. Cunningham (1883): 49.
44. Srinivasan (2007): 71.
45. Falk and Bennett (2009).
46. Cunningham (1883): 52.
47. Sachau (1910b): 6.
48. Smith (1915): 74.
49. Falk (2001).
50. Cunningham (1883): 53-57.
51. Cunningham (1883): 63.
52. Sachau (1910b): 5.
53. Sircar (1965): 297.

"And all who told it added something new, and all who heard it, made enlargements too."

- Alexander Pope

3. THE LEGENDS OF VIKRAMĀDITYA

Indian tradition recognizes Emperor Vikramāditya as the greatest ruler of India. The Vikrama era of 57 BCE constituted in his memory continues to be used in India symbolizing the love and affection people have for him even though more than 2000 years have passed since he left this mortal world. Modern history has denied the very existence of this great emperor and some minor king named Azes has been credited for instituting the Vikrama era. Even though the Vikrama era deserved to be the national era of India after independence, this honour was given to Śaka era, an era that modern historians have given credit to a foreign ruler for instituting it. It comes as no surprise that invader-loving historians of India will choose an era they think to have been instituted by a foreigner over an era that stands so tall over all other eras that its choice as national era should have required no thinking at all. Let us therefore consider in full the exploits of the real Emperor Vikramāditya, and hope that this historical blunder will be corrected and Vikrama era will receive the official honour that it deserves.

There are a number of legends about Vikramāditya that have made him the darling of the masses. Some of these legends are based on historical persons, and some of them have other meanings behind them. In this chapter we will analyze the legends that do not have any historical interpretation. In the next three chapters we will discuss the legends that relate to historical Vikramādityas. We then conclude with the exploits of the Vikramāditya in whose honour the Vikrama era has been instituted.

The memory of Vikramāditya has been preserved in the literary traditions of Hindus such as the Gāthāsaptaśatī composed by Hāla Sātavāhana, Bṛhatkathā composed by Guṇāḍhya, Bṛhatkathāmañjarī composed by Kṣemendra, and Kathāsaritsāgara composed by Somadeva. The last two texts are based on Bṛhatkathā, which was originally written in Paiśāchī Prākṛta and is not available now. The adventures of Vikramāditya have been popularized in a number of books of fiction such as Vetālapañchaviṃśati (popularly known as Vetāla Pachīsī), Siṃhāsana-dwātṛṃśikā (popularly known as Siṃhāsana Battīsī) and Śuka-saptaśatī (popularly known as the story of the "Parrot and Mynah").

The story of Vikramāditya and his family is described in many Jain texts such as Paṭṭāvalīs, Harivaṃśa, and Prabhāvakacharita composed by Prabhāchandra, Prabandhakoṣa composed by Rājaśekhara, Prabandha Chintāmaṇi composed by Merutuṅga Sūri, Purātana Prabandha Saṃgraha and Vikrama Charitra composed by Devamūrti, Vikrama Charitra composed by Śubhaśīla, and Vikrama Pañchadaṇḍa Prabandha composed by Rāmachandra Sūri. Most historians consider the story of Kālakāchārya and Vikramāditya to be historical, which in fact is allegorical and has a very deep scientific meaning.

3.1 The Time Lord

Jain texts contain the story of a teacher named Kālakāchārya and Vikramāditya that goes as follows [1]:

> *"A Sanskrit treatise of 10 pages entitled Kālakāchārya Kathā, without date, and without the author's name, contains the following story:*
>
> *In the town of Dharāvāsa there was a king of the name of Vajra Sinha. His queen's name was Sura Sundarī. They had a son named Kālaka Sūri (in some MSS. the name is spelt Kālika Sūri) and a daughter Saraswatī.*
>
> *Kālaka was initiated into the Jain doctrines by Guna Sundara Sūri, and Saraswatī was initiated by Kālaka. They went to Avanti or Ujjayinī in Malwa. Saraswatī whilst walking with other Sadhvis, or nuns, outside the city, was seen by Gardabhilla, Rājā of Ujjayinī, who became enamoured of her beauty. He caused her to be carried by force into his Antahpura or zenana. Kālakāchārya proceeded to the king, and entreated for the release of his sister, who had vowed perpetual chastity. He appealed to his duty as king to afford protection against violence and injustice, and had recourse to other arguments, but the king was inexorable and made no reply. Kālakāchārya then complained to the Sangha or congregation, which also interfered and tried in many ways to persuade the king to release the nun. The king paid no heed to the Sangha also. At last Kālakāchārya, in despair, determined on revenge, and to do his utmost to deprive the king and his sons of the throne and all its privileges. He feigned madness, rubbed mud on his body, and commenced wandering through Ujjayinī. The old ministers of the king entreated him thereon to release the nun, but without success. Kālaka Sūri, on this, proceeded to the west bank of the Indus. The kings of the country were called Sāhi. He resided at the house of one of the greatest Sāhis. By his skill in astrology he obtained great influence over the Sāhi. One day finding the Sāhi dejected, Kālakāchārya inquired into the cause. The Sāhi replied, "Our King,*

who is called Sāhina-Sāhi, has written to me to send off my head at once, and a similar order has been sent to 95 other rajas or chiefs." Kālakāchārya advised that they should all join their forces and invade Hindūkadeśa (India). They gladly adopted the idea, crossed the Sindhu (Indus) and proceeded to Surāshtra, where they halted on account of the rainy season. All the chiefs, hands folded, served Kālakāchārya as their Guru (preceptor). After the rains, the Guru recommended them to march on Avanti-deśa (Malwa), and after defeating Raja Gardabhilla, to divide his kingdom amongst themselves. They pleaded that they had no more of the sinews of war. Kālakāchārya, by a mysterious or magic rite furnished them with gold bricks. The Rajas then beating the Nobata (drum) reached Lāta (Broach). They took the Rajas of Lāta, named Balamitra and Bhanumitra with them, and appeared on the confines of Avanti-deśa (Malwa). The Raja of Avanti proceeded to the threatened spot. The two armies fought with Kunta (spears?) and bows. Finding his army defeated, he retreated secretly to Visālā-purī (Ujjayinī). The enemy's force thereon laid siege to the city. One day, no fight taking place, the Sāhibhatas (Sahi warriors) inquired of Kālakāchārya the reason of the cessation of hostilities. Kālakāchārya replied, this day is the 8th of the moon, and the king of Avanti is trying to attain Gardabhī Vidya (Gardabhī science). On searching they found the Gardabha, (she-ass) entering a house in the bazaar, which fact was communicated to the Guru. At each braying, 108 archers were killed. On this the Guru, who was light and quick of hand, himself approached the ass with bow and arrows, and told the chiefs that when the she-ass opened her mouth, to choke it with instruments of war. They did accordingly, when the she-ass, having covered Kālakāchārya's head with her solid and liquid product disappeared. The disappearance of the animal deprived the king Gardabhilla of all energy; and Sāhi Rajas, having secured his person, carried him to the feet of Kālakāchārya, when Gardabhilla stood with his looks cast down to earth. Kālakāchārya reproached him for his evil conduct, and said that he had that day met with the fruit of the tree of the sin of destroying the vows of a religious lady. Leave your evil

> *ways, and embrace virtues yet – declared Kālakāchārya. The king was not pleased with the Munindra's charge, and having been untied was set at liberty. Saraswatī re-entered on her pure (charitra) course. The Sāhi at whose house Kālakāchārya had put up became the President of the chiefs, and was put in possession of (the city), and others appropriated to themselves different portions of the country. This is the "Śaka Vansa" (Scythian race or dynasty). Kālakāchārya having undergone the rite of confession, delighted the Sangha.... Vikrama flourished 470 years after Vīra, and the Sāki Rājya lasted 17 years, when Vikramāditya, having destroyed the Śakas, regained his kingdom. One hundred and thirty-five years afterwards a Śaka king again flourished."*

Every historian considers this story to be historical, so we need not provide any reference to this effect. However, this story has a scientific meaning and has hardly anything to do with history. This story symbolizes the effort to preserve scientific knowledge in the form of popular tradition, which is a hallmark of Jainism and Hinduism. Jains had mastered the science of astronomy and Hindus adopted many of their models as their own. The story of Vikramāditya was conceived and popularized by Jains, but over time Vikramāditya became an iconic figure for Hindus too.

Vikramāditya was conceived by Jains as the legendary king of Ujjain, known in ancient times as Ujjayinī, which was the capital of the Malwa region. From time immemorial, this city was the centre of religio-cultural activities of India. It was known as Anādi Ujjayinī, a city without beginning in time. Ujjayinī received several names over time, one of which was Avantikā for being the capital of the kingdom of Avanti. Avantikā is among the seven holy cities, which are considered the doorway to salvation, according to Hindu scriptures. Another name for Ujjain was Viśālā, a name by which Kālidāsa refers to this city in Meghaduta. He says, "O Cloud, when you go to Avanti, go to the city of Viśālā, where elders tell the story of Udayana. This city looks like a gleaming part of heaven that people from heaven have brought with them with their remaining meritorious deeds." The story of Udayana, the daring king of Vatsa, and Vāsavadattā, the ethereally beautiful princess of Avanti, is the most endearing love story of ancient India, which formed the basis of many literary works. A time long ago, Ujjayinī was considered to be at the centre of the universe. We can't be sure of that, but Ujjayinī certainly is located at a very special place in India. It was realized very early in the history of India that Ujjayinī was located at the Tropic of Cancer. It was this location at the Tropic of Cancer that formed the basis of the legend of Vikramāditya.

Traditionally, it is assumed that the word Vikramāditya is composed by joining the words "Vikrama" and "Āditya". Vikrama means valour, and Āditya means Sun, and thus the meaning of Vikramāditya is the "Sun of Valour" or "Brave as the Sun". However, this was not the intended meaning behind the legend of Vikramāditya. The word Vikramāditya can also be composed by joining the prefix "Vi" with the words "Krama" and "Āditya". The prefix "Vi" imparts the meaning of deviation to the word that follows it. For example, the word "Vikāra" means creating deviation and hence connotes degradation. The word "Krama" means "order" and "Āditya" of course means Sun. Putting it all together, Vikramāditya means deviation in the order of the Sun. Let us ponder at what happens to the Sun at Ujjayinī: during the summer months, the Sun moves northwards towards Ujjayinī and continues till the day of the summer solstice, on which day the Sun stands vertically up at Ujjayinī. The next day the Sun reverses its journey and starts going south. This fact that the Sun changes its course at Ujjayinī, formed the basis of the legend of Vikramāditya. It was because of its location at the Tropic of Cancer that Ujjayinī became the most prominent centre for astronomical research in ancient India. It also became the place from which time was synchronized all over India. It became the prime meridian of the ancient world in the manner of Greenwich today. Bhāskara-I has written that the prime meridian passes through Laṅkā, Vātsyapura, Avantī, Sthāneśvara, and abode of the gods [2]. Other ancient Indian astronomers have specified many other points on this meridian, and so there is no doubt about the intended meaning. Here, the abode of the gods is Mount Meru, which is the astronomical term for the North Pole. Laṅkā here does not represent any city in Sri Lanka, but a point at the intersection of the equator and the meridian passing through Ujjain. This point is in the Indian Ocean, far away from Sri Lanka. As time all over India was synchronized from the time in Ujjayinī, the Lord of Ujjayinī was made Mahākāla or "Time, the Great" from Mahā meaning "great" and Kāla meaning "time". Ujjayinī is famous for the temple of Mahākāla, who is identified with Lord Śiva now.

With this background, it is easy to see that the story of Kālakāchārya is based on this astronomical understanding. Kālakāchārya is made by joining words Kālaka and Āchārya. Kālaka or Kāla means "time", and Āchārya means "teacher". So Kālakāchārya is "teacher time" or time itself. His mother's name was Sura Sundarī, which means beautiful like a goddess. His teacher's name was Guna Sundara, which means good quality. Both these names are based on qualities and are not really proper names, which further supports the thesis that this is an allegorical story and not history. The sister of Kālakāchārya was named Saraswatī, who is the Goddess of Learning, again not a personal name. If there was still any doubt, it is completely erased by the name of the king of Ujjayinī, which is given as Gardabhilla. Gardabhilla is a play on the word Gardabha, which means donkey. Why would a king call himself a donkey? Not even a common man does that. Again, there is a purpose behind choosing a donkey to represent the king of Ujjayinī. Donkeys have a gestation period of 365.2 days and thus donkey represents a year in the ancient Indian system of knowledge. Thus the whole story represents the knowledge about measurement of time from the city of Ujjayinī, which was based on it being on the prime meridian, and at the Tropic of Cancer. As I have shown in the last chapter that Mālava era has a starting point of 702 BCE and Ujjayinī was the capital of the Malwa region, it follows that this astronomical understanding was already in place in the eighth century BCE. Over the next several centuries the popularity of this saga continued to grow. After this title was adopted by emperors, many more legends were added to the original saga. Some of these stories have a historical basis and some of them don't. For now, we will take up another Vikramāditya story that is not historical but allegorical and involves two popular eras, both of which gained their popularity from the demolition of the Śakas.

3.2 A Tale of Two Eras

This is another Jain story that involves Vikramāditya and Śālivāhana as main protagonists. Burgess has recounted the story [3]:

> *"Here the great king Śālivāhana, who founded the Śaka era, is said to have been born and ruled in the first century. Legend says he was the son of a foreign Brāhmaṇī girl, who lodged with her brothers in the house of a kumbhāra or potter, and his supernatural father was Śesha, the king of Pātāla, the region of the Nāga or serpent race: but other legends make him the foster child of king Dīpakaṃi. As a boy he played the part of a young Cyrus among his companions. When the great Vikramāditya of Ujjain, after a long reign, perceived omens of evil and concluded from them that his end was near, he ordered his Vetāla to find out whether an infant existed anywhere, born of a mother two years of age, for only by such a child had Śiva revealed that he should be slain. At Pratishṭhāna the Vetāla found at the door of a potter's house a young girl playing with a boy who answered the conditions. When Vikramāditya heard that the child boding evil for him had been discovered, he*

> *resolved to slay it. Marching with an army to Pratishṭhāna, he challenged Śālivāhana to fight. Nāgendra (the king of serpents), however, had arrived and communicated to him a mantra or magical formula, whereby he might obtain whatever he wanted; accordingly Śālivāhana transmuted clay figures of elephants, horses, and soldiers into living ones, with whom he gave battle to his enemy, and finally defeated him. Vikrama fled to Ujjayinī, and left Sātavāhana, as he is also called, king in Pratishṭhāna, which became "a rich city, having wide roads, large temples and private dwellings, brilliantly white markets, fortifications and ditches; and Sātavāhana having made all the people of Dakshināpatha free from debt, and conquered the country as far as the Tāpī, introduced his own era therein." This era is known as the Śaka era, and dates from the coronation of Śālivāhana: the first year beginning at the vernal equinox, A.D. 79."*

This is the story of the battle between two eras to gain popularity. The Vikrama era has the starting point of 57 BCE and Śālivāhana era has the starting point of 78 CE. There is a difference of 135 years between the starting points of these two eras. Clearly Vikramāditya was not alive when the Śālivāhana era was founded. In fact, the Vikrama era starts with the death of Vikramāditya in 57 BCE. Since both of these eras were very popular, a story has been constructed to depict the struggle for supremacy between these two eras. Historically, Vikramāditya and Śālivāhana never came face to face.

Over the course of history, a number of emperors took the title of Vikramāditya. After its original conception, the next stage in the Vikramāditya saga unfolded when the Imperial Gupta emperor Samudragupta took control of Malwa and adopted the title Vikramāditya. After him, this title was also taken by his son Chandragupta II. Skandagupta, grandson of Chandragupta II, was the next to take this title. These mighty emperors of the Imperial Gupta dynasty gave rise to many legends of Vikramāditya. After them, this title was taken by the emperor after whom the Vikrama era was instituted. With so many historical Vikramādityas, in addition to the legendary Vikramāditya just discussed, a whole lot of confusion has been created. We will deal with the different stories about Vikramādityas in the next three chapters and clear the confusion by assigning to each Vikramāditya the saga that belongs to them individually.

Notes

1. Dāji (1872).
2. Laghubhāskarīya 1.23.
3. Burgess (1878): 55.

"It is essential to the idea of a law, that it be attended with a sanction; or, in other words, a penalty or punishment for disobedience. If there be no penalty annexed to disobedience, the resolutions or commands which pretend to be laws will, in fact, amount to nothing more than advice or recommendation. This penalty, whatever it may be, can only be inflicted in two ways: by the agency of the Courts and Ministers of Justice, or by military force; by the coercion of the magistracy, or by the coercion of arms. The first kind can evidently apply only to men: the last kind must, of necessity, be employed against bodies politic, or communities, or States."

- Alexander Hamilton

4. MIGHT OF THE EAGLES

In the fourth century BCE, North India was divided into many small kingdoms. However, India was culturally united and its people took extreme pride in belonging to the land they considered coveted by the Gods. Nāgas were a powerful force in North India, while Vākāṭakas ruled from South India. A marriage alliance took place between the Nāgas and the the Vākāṭakas to present a united front in response to the impending invasion by Alexander. Further east, the Guptas were ruling in Magadha south of the Ganges, while a powerful Vajji confederation including Lichchhavis was ruling north of the Ganges from Vaiśālī. A second marriage alliance took place between the Guptas and the Lichchhavis to present a second wall of defence. Let us start by getting familiar with one of the most enigmatic people of ancient India, the Nāgas.

4.1 The Deadly Nāgas

The Nāgas were one of the original inhabitants of India. In the aftermath of the Mahābhārata war, the Vedic Aryans of Indus Valley Civilization moved into different areas from their original home in current day North-western India and Pakistan. Their westward migration gave rise to Vedic Aryan colonies in Persia, Central Asia, and later Europe. Their eastward migration brought them face to face with the mighty Nāgas.

A lot of confusion exists regarding the history of the Nāgas. Just like the stories of Vikramāditya, cosmological, astronomical and the apparent meaning of Nāga have become enmeshed with the historical stories of the Nāgas. This web of fact and myths needs to be carefully disentangled to uncover the real history of the Nāgas.

The apparent meaning of Nāga is a cobra, and this has prompted the depiction of the Nāgas as cobras. However, the Nāgas were real people, and it is obvious from the marriage of the Nāga princesses with Vākāṭaka and Gupta rulers. The depiction of human Nāgas as cobras has given rise to the story of shape-shifting cobras in the popular imagination. Ichchhādhārī Nāgas, as they are called, have the ability to change to human form from the cobra form and vice-versa. These shape-shifting Nāgas are supposed to guard fabulous treasures, which probably has its origin in the Nāga kings amassing huge fortunes.

Another popular myth based on this depiction is that of Viṣakanyās, i.e. poison-girls. Viṣakanyās were very pretty girls, who were administered poison since childhood in slowly increasing quantities. They were so full of venom by the time they became adult that if they kissed someone, that person would die immediately. They were sent to rival kings to present the kiss of death. As the Hindus, Jains and Buddhists vied for the allegiance of the Nāgas, they are often depicted as providing protective cover by fully extending their hoods in Hindu, Jain and Buddhist motifs.

Nāga history is often traced to Śeṣa Nāga. Śeṣa Nāga has a cosmological meaning, which is apparent from the name Śeṣa Nāga itself. Śeṣa means "remaining/remainder" and thus Śeṣa Nāga represents the unmanifested universe or what lies outside of the universe. Our universe, the manifested universe, is represented by Lord Viṣṇu and his avatars -- Lord Rāma and Lord Kṛṣṇa. Lord Rāma's brother Lakṣmaṇa, and Lord Kṛṣṇa's brother Balarāma are considered to be the incarnations of Śeṣa Nāga. It was common to depict Balarāma as a cobra in the city of Mathura, which was one of the major centres of Nāga power.

A prominent Nāga king in the epics is Nahuṣa, who was made the ruler of heaven -- Indra, when the previous Indra had run away. Nahuṣa was cursed by the seven sages to fall to earth in serpent form after he insulted them in his bid to obtain the pleasure of Śachī, the previous Indra's wife. As Indra also means Sun, and the seven sages are prominent actors in this story, the hidden meaning of this story is obviously astronomical.

After Śeṣa Nāga and Nahuṣa, the most prominent Nāgas in the epics are Vāsuki and Takṣaka. Vāsuki is the Nāga, who is coiled around Lord Śiva's neck. He was also used for churning of the ocean by the gods and demons by wrapping him around the Mandāra Mountain. In Buddhist mythology, Vāsuki is one of the eight great Nāga kings, and he frequently appears in the audience during Buddha's sermons. It is obvious from the nature of these stories that Vāsuki Nāga was not a historical person.

This brings us to the Nāga king Takṣaka, the ruler of the ancient city of Takṣaśilā, which was famous for the university named after it. As Vedic Aryans moved eastward after the Mahābhārata war and looked for suitable places to settle, they ventured into lands already inhabited by the Nāgas. The clash between the Vedic Aryans and the Nāgas has been preserved in a cryptic form in a story from the Mahābhārata. The story told in the Ādi Parva of Mahābhārata is as follows: One day king Parīkṣita, son of

Abhimanyu and grandson of Arjuna, pierced a deer with a sharp arrow. Even though wounded, the deer ran for its life in the deep forest and soon went out of sight. Parīkṣita tried to follow the deer and came to a sage deep in meditation. Parīkṣita asked the sage about the deer, but got no answer as the sage had taken the vow of silence. In frustration, Parīkṣita placed a dead snake around the neck of the sage and left. That sage had a son named Śṛṅgī, who became very angry when he saw his father in such condition. He cursed that within seven days Parīkṣita would die of a bite by Takṣaka, king of the Nāgas. When Śṛṅgī told this to his father Śamīka, who had now broken his vow of silence, he said to his enraged son that ascetics should not act like this. The king has protected us righteously and should have been forgiven. If you destroy Dharma, Dharma will verily destroy you, the sage cautioned. The king was fatigued and hungry and did not know of my vow of silence. A country without a king suffers from evils. The king punishes the offenders and the fear of punishment is conducive to peace. Śṛṅgī said that even though he had acted improperly, his curse would not go void.

Śamīka then sent one of his disciples to king Parīkṣita to explain what had happened. Parīkṣita repented his action and consulted his ministers. A mansion was erected on a solitary column and the king lived in there guarded from all sides. On the seventh day, Takṣaka sent snakes disguised as ascetics to offer fruits, flower and water urgently. Takṣaka had hidden himself in a fruit and bit the king before the Sun had set on the seventh day. After the death of king Parīkṣita, his minor son Janamejaya was made king. When he became an adult, Janamejaya asked his councillors how his father had died. After the councillors narrated the whole story to Janamejaya, he vowed to take revenge for the murder of his father.

Janamejaya then started a snake sacrifice in which he determined to burn all the snakes, including Takṣaka. As the sacrificial priests poured clarified butter in the burning fire and chanted the mantras, snakes started to fall from the sky into the blazing fire. Takṣaka sought protection from Indra, who provided him refuge. The Nāga king Vāsuki then sent his sister's son Āstika to pacify Janamejaya and stop the snake sacrifice. As the sacrifice continued, Indra himself started to get pulled into the fire, and at this point he abandoned Takṣaka to save himself. As Takṣaka was about to fall in the sacrificial fire, Janamejaya requested Āstika to ask for whatever he desired. Āstika asked for the sacrifice to come to an end and let no more snakes be sacrificed. Janamejaya repeatedly asked him to take something else, but Āstika persisted and the snake sacrifice came to an end.

Takṣaka seems to be the titular name of the king of the Nāgas, as we also have another story about Nāga king Takṣaka in the Mahābhārata, but this time it involves Arjuna, grandfather of Parīkṣita. In this story, Arjuna and Kṛṣṇa were approached by an aged Brāhmaṇa for help. Upon further inquiry, the aged Brāhmaṇa turned out to be the fire god Agni, who had fallen ill and needed to burn the Khāṇḍava forest to satisfy his hunger and regain his health. Upon being asked why Agni needed help in doing what came naturally to him, Agni replied that the Khāṇḍava forest was home to Takṣaka, who was friend of Indra, the rain god. As soon as Agni started to burn the Khāṇḍava forest, Indra soaked the forest with rain and stopped him from burning the forest. Arjuna covered the forest with a roof of arrows, thereby allowing Agni to burn the Khāṇḍava forest. Indra came to rescue the forest, but was beaten by Arjuna and had to retreat. As the Khāṇḍava forest burned, Takṣaka tried to escape. Agni followed him, but Takṣaka somehow managed to save his life.

It seems that Khāṇḍava forest was the original home of Takṣaka and his Nāga subjects. Arjuna wanted to clear this forest to construct the city of Indraprastha, where present day Delhi is located. Takṣaka and his subjects resisted, but ultimately had to run away. A few decades later, another Takṣaka, possibly the grandson of the original Takṣaka found an opportunity to corner Parīkṣita by dressing the Nāgas as Brāhmaṇas and killed him to avenge the destruction of his ancestral home. When Janamejaya grew up and came to know of the treachery committed by Takṣaka, he vowed revenge and attacked the Nāgas. A number of Nāgas were killed in the attack, but a truce was called before Takṣaka could be captured. It seems that after running away from the burning Khāṇḍava forest, Takṣaka moved far northwest from Khāṇḍava forest and founded the city of Takṣaśilā, current day Taxila in Pakistan. Janamejaya attacked Takṣaśilā to take revenge and conquered it. The victory of Janamejaya over Takṣaśilā has been mentioned in the Mahābhārata [1].

A long time later, possibly over one and half millennia, if the Mahābhārata war took place close to 1900 BCE, we find a number of Nāga kings ruling in North India before the rise of the Imperial Guptas. By this time, they were fully in the Hindu fold and many of them were staunch devotees of Lord Śiva. We find the following information in the Chammak copper plate inscription of the Vākāṭaka king Pravarasena II [2]:

> *"... Who was the son of the Mahārāja of the Vākāṭakas, the illustrious Rudrasena-I, who was an excessively devout devotee of (the god) Svāmī-Mahābhairava; who was the daughter's son of the illustrious Bhavanāga, the Mahārāja of the Bhāraśivas, whose royal line owed its origin to the great satisfaction of (the god) Śiva, (caused) by (their) carrying a liṅga of Śiva placed as a load upon (their) shoulders, (and) who were besprinkled on the forehead with the pure water of (the) river Bhāgīrathī that had been obtained by (their) valour, and (who) performed ablutions after the celebration of ten asvamedha sacrifices; ..."*

According to this inscription, Bhāraśiva Nāgas received their name due to carrying a liṅga of Śiva on their shoulders and their kings had performed ten Aśvamedha sacrifices on the banks of the Ganges. It seems reasonable to assume that the famous

Daśaśvamedha Ghāṭa in Varanasi received its name from the performance of ten Aśvamedha sacrifices by Bhāraśiva Nāga kings.

A number of Nāga kings were ruling in North India before the rise of the Imperial Guptas, according to the Purāṇas [3]:

> *"Hear also the future kings of Vidiśā. Bhogin, son of the Naga king Śeṣa, will be king, conqueror of his enemies' cities, a king who will exalt the Nāga family. Sadāchandra, and Chandrāṃśa who will be a second Nakhavant, then Dhanadharman, and Vaṅgara is remembered as the fourth. Then Bhūtinanda will reign in the Vaidiśa kingdom. ... Nine Nāka kings will enjoy the city Champāvatī; and 7 Nāgas will enjoy the charming city Mathura. Kings born of the Gupta race will enjoy all these territories, namely, along the Ganges, Prayāga, Sāketa, and the Magadhas."*

The above text shows that Vidiśā, Champāvatī and Mathurā were three centres of Nāga power. Elsewhere in the Purāṇas, Padmāvatī and Kāntipurī are also described as seats of Nāga power. Mathurā is a well known city in Uttar Pradesh. Vidisha is a city in Madhya Pradesh about 60 km northeast of Bhopal, the capital city of Madhya Pradesh. During the medieval times, this city was known as Bhilsa. Champāvatī is the same as Padmāvatī [4]. Alexander Cunningham had wrongly identified Padmāvatī with Narwar near Gwalior, but was corrected by M.B. Garde, who identified Padmāvatī with Pawaya, also known as Padam Pawaya [5]. Pawaya is about 70 km south of Gwalior in Madhya Pradesh. Kantipurī is the village of Kotwal, about 40 km north of Gwalior [6]. Thus the four major centres of the Nāga power -- Vidiśā, Padmāvatī (Champāvatī), Kāntipurī and Mathura -- covered a large part of North India, and the marriage of the daughter of Bhāraśiva Nāga king Bhavanāga with Vākāṭaka crown prince Gautamīputra from Deccan around 330 BCE resulted in a formidable confederation to take on the impending invasion of India by Alexander. Luckily, Alexander was sent packing by the fearless

Porus. The alliance of the Nāgas and Vākāṭakas continued for about 20 years, when in a series of rapid attacks Nāgas were completely overwhelmed by the Imperial Guptas.

4.2 The Imperial Guptas

The first known ruler of the Imperial Gupta dynasty was Gupta, who was followed by Ghaṭotkachagupta. Around 330 BCE, Chandragupta I, son of Ghaṭotkachagupta, was married to the Lichchhavi princess Kumāradevī, which greatly enhanced the power and prestige of the Guptas. It was this marriage alliance that changed the fortunes of the Guptas. A year later Kumāradevī gave birth to Samudragupta, who later united most of India under one rule and was the first emperor to take the title of Vikramāditya. Chandragupta was a young man in his early twenties when the forces of Alexander reached the borders of India in 327 BCE. Chandragupta left his toddler son Samudragupta in the care of his family to get the first-hand account of the threat posed by Alexander. Soon, he met Porus and urged him to fight Alexander with all his might. He then enlisted himself in Alexander's army and encouraged fellow Indians to rebel against Alexander. We have the following account of the meeting of Chandragupta with Alexander by the Greek classical writer Justin [7]:

> *"Seleucus Nicator waged many wars in the east after the partition of Alexander's empire among his generals. He first took Babylon, and then with his forces augmented by victory subjugated the Bactrians. He then passed over into India, which after Alexander's death, as if the yoke of servitude had been shaken off from its neck, had put his prefects to death. Sandrocottus as the leader who achieved their freedom, but after his victory he forfeited by his tyranny all title to the name of liberator, for he oppressed with servitude the very people whom he had emancipated from foreign thraldom. He was born in humble life, but was prompted to aspire to royalty by an omen significant of an august destiny. For when by*

his insolent behaviour he had offended Alexandrum, and was ordered by that king to be put to death, he sought safety by a speedy flight. When he lay down overcome with fatigue and had fallen into a deep sleep, a lion of enormous size approaching the slumberer licked with its tongue the sweat which oozed profusely from his body, and when he awoke, quietly took its departure. It was this prodigy which first inspired him with the hope of winning the throne, and so having collected a band of robbers, he instigated the Indians to overthrow the existing government. When he was thereafter preparing to attack Alexander's prefects, a wild elephant of monstrous size approached him, and kneeling submissively like a tame elephant received him on to its back and fought vigorously in front of the army. Sandrocottus having thus won the throne was reigning over India when Seleucus was laying the foundations of his future greatness. Seleucus having made a treaty with him and otherwise settled his affairs in the east, returned home to prosecute the war with Antigonus."

Further light on the meeting of Chandragupta with Alexander is thrown by the Greek classical writer Plutarch [8]:

"Alexander at first in vexation and rage withdrew to his tent, and shutting himself up lay there feeling no gratitude towards those who had thwarted his purpose of crossing the Ganges; but regarding a retreat as tantamount to a confession of defeat. But being swayed by the persuasions of his friends, and the entreaties of his soldiers who stood weeping and lamenting at the door of his tent, he at last relented, and prepared to retreat. He first, however, contrived many unfair devices to exalt his fame among the natives, as, for instance, causing arms for men and stalls and bridles for horses to be made much beyond the usual size, and these he left scattered about. He also erected altars for the gods which the kings of the Praisiai even to the present day hold in veneration, crossing the river to offer sacrifices upon them in the Hellenic fashion. Androkottos himself, who was then but a youth, saw Alexander himself, and afterwards used to declare that Alexander could easily have taken possession of

the whole country since the king was hated and despised by his subjects for the wickedness of his disposition and the meanness of his origin."

After Alexander's devastating defeat at the hands of Porus, Chandragupta returned from the border. Now he was even more resolved to bring India under a unifying force to thwart any future invasion. He started to build his forces for this purpose. He received assistance from his in-laws, who united under his banner. To the west, the confederation of the Nāgas and the Vākāṭakas posed a formidable challenge and Chandragupta had to wait a while for an opportune moment. Under the leadership of his father Ghaṭotkachagupta, he started to slowly expand his territory and consolidate his forces with the help of the Vajji confederation of which his in-laws Lichchhavis were an important part.

4.3 The Vajji Confederation

Vajji or Vṛji region was the area east of the river Gaṇḍaka, west of the river Koshi, north of the Ganges and south of Nepal. The Vajji state was a republic consisting of a confederacy of eight clans. Four major clans of this confederacy were Videha, Lichchhavi, Jñātrika and Vṛji. The names of other four clans are lost to us. The capital of Vajji republic was located at Vaiśālī, which is present day Basarh in the state of Bihar, about 35 km southwest of Muzaffarpur. Videha was an ancient kingdom, with its capital at Mithilā. The kings of Videha kept the title of Janak.

The Vajji confederation was formed after the fall of the kingdom of Videha. Around 330 BCE, Chandragupta I, son of Ghaṭotkachagupta, was married to the Lichchhavi princess Kumāradevī in response to the impending invasion by Alexander, and the marriage alliance between the Nāgas and Vākāṭakas. When the Imperial Guptas became the paramount power of India, Lichchhavis were emboldened to venture further north to Nepal. In the light of the chronology developed in this book, the history of

Nepal will also need to undergo serious revision as the Lichchhavis came to Nepal six centuries before what is believed currently. The marriage alliance between the Guptas and Lichchhavis proved to be of great benefit to both and from this marriage alliance was born one of the greatest emperors of India and the first historical emperor to assume the title of Vikramāditya.

4.4 Samudragupta the Great

During the time of consolidation of Gupta power, Chandragupta-I paid special attention in grooming Samudragupta to be a formidable warrior. Finally, around 310 BCE, the opportunity arrived for which the Guptas were waiting for a long time. With the death of the Vākāṭaka king Pravarasena I in 310 BCE, there was a struggle for the throne. Vākāṭaka power was divided and a separate branch of Vākāṭakas was established at Vatsagulma. The Nāgas could not remain neutral in this fight for succession among the Vākāṭakas, and the Nāga unity was broken. Samudragupta, now about 19-years-old, led the army under the command of his father Chandragupta-I, and challenged the Nāgas in a series of rapid attacks. He came down heavily on the Nāga kings and exterminated them before they had a chance to regroup. To celebrate this grand achievement, Chandragupta-I was handed over the reigns of the now expanded Gupta kingdom by his overjoyed father Ghaṭotkachagupta in 309 BCE. Over 50 years later Chandragupta II, the grandson of Chandragupta-I, who was named after him, honoured his grandfather by counting the dates of the Gupta era from the day of the coronation of his grandfather Chandragupta-I. At the time of coronation of Chandragupta-I, Samudragupta was about 20 years old and bubbling with energy to take over the world. By 305 BCE, he had extended Chandragupta's empire to the borders of India. This is the time, Seleucus, who was one of the commanders under Alexander and had taken over part of Alexander's empire, attacked India to seek revenge for

Alexander's defeat. However, Seleucus was defeated after a prolonged war and made a pact by offering his daughter in marriage to Samudragupta, who was of marriageable age at that time. Seleucus also ceded territories to Chandragupta that extended his empire all the way to present day Afghanistan. In return, Seleucus received 500 war elephants from Chandragupta, which helped him in defeating his rivals. Greek historian Plutarch has given the following account of the meeting of Chandragupta and Seleucus [9]:

> *"The battle with Poros depressed the spirits of the Macedonians, and made them very unwilling to advance farther into India. For as it was with the utmost difficulty they had beaten him when the army he led amounted only to 20,000 infantry and 2000 cavalry, they now most resolutely opposed Alexander when he insisted that they should cross the Ganges. This river, they heard, had a breadth of two-and-thirty stadia, and a depth of 100 fathoms, while its farther banks were covered all over with armed men, horses, and elephants. For the kings of the Gandaritai and the Praisiai were reported to be waiting for him with an army of 80,000 horse, 200,000 foot, 8000 war chariots, and 6000 fighting elephants. Nor was this any exaggeration, for not long afterwards Androkottos, who had by that time mounted the throne, presented Seleukos with 500 elephants, and overran and subdued the whole of India with an army of 600,000 men."*

Greek classical writer Strabo has given the following account of the pact between Chandragupta and Seleucus [10]:

> *"The Indus runs in a parallel course along the breadth of these regions. The Indians possess partly some of the countries lying along Indus, but these belonged formerly to the Persians. Alexander took them away from the Arianoi and established in them colonies of his own. Seleukos Nikator gave them to Sandrokottus in concluding a marriage alliance, and received in exchange 500 elephants."*

We need to keep in mind here that Greek writers do not specify who was married to whom. Since Seleucus lost the war, it is assumed that he offered his daughter in marriage to conclude the alliance. Looking at this evidence in conjunction with the proud declaration of Samudragupta in the Eran Stone inscription, we realize that the daughter of Seleucus was married to Samudragupta.

In the Eran Stone Inscription, Samudragupta claims to have earned his wife using his prowess [11]:

> *"(L. 9.) - ...there was Samudragupta, equal to (the gods) Dhanada and Antaka in (respectively) pleasure and anger; . . . by policy; (and) [by whom] the whole tribe of kings upon the earth was [overthrown] and reduced to the loss of the wealth of their sovereignty; ...*
>
> *(L. 17.) - [By whom] there was married a virtuous and faithful wife, whose dower was provided by (his) manliness and prowess; who was possessed of an abundance of [elephants] and horses and money and grain; who delighted in the houses of . . . ; (and) who went about in the company of many sons and sons' sons...*

The exact words used in the inscription are "pauruṣa-parākrama-datta-śulkā" meaning whose nuptial gift was paid by manliness and prowess. Samudragupta's wife was named Dattadevī. The first part of the name "Datta" means given, as in given by her father due to defeat in war. The second part Devī is simply an honorific for a lady. Thus, Dattadevī was not her name before marriage, but given after marriage, according to the circumstances. We are fortunate to have received a very good account of the heroic deeds of the great emperor Samudragupta in the Allahabad Stone Pillar inscription as follows [12]:

> *(Line 29.) - This lofty column (is) as it were an arm of the earth, proclaiming the fame,-which, having pervaded the entire surface of the earth with (its) development that was caused by (his) conquest of the whole world, (has departed) hence (and now) experiences the sweet happiness attained by (his) having gone to the abode of*

(Indra) the lord of the gods,-of the Mahārājādhirāja, the glorious Samudragupta,

(L. 1.) - [Who] . . . by his own kinsmen . . . ; whose . . .

(L. 3.) - [Who] . . . twanging (of the bow-string) . . . burst open and scattered . . . dishevelled . . .

(L. 5.) - Whose happy mind was accustomed to associate with learned people; who was the supporter of the real truth of the scriptures; . . . firmly fixed . . . .who, having overwhelmed, with the (force of the) commands of the collective merits of (his) learned men, those things which obstruct the beauty of excellent poetry, (still) enjoys, in the world of the wise, the sovereignty of the fame (produced) by much poetry, . . . and of clear meaning. . .

(L 7.) - Who, being looked at (with envy) by the faces, melancholy (through the rejection of themselves), of others of equal birth, while the attendants of the court breathed forth deep sighs (of happiness), was bidden by (his) father,-who, exclaiming "Verily (he is) worthy," embraced (him) with the hairs of (his) body standing erect (through pleasure) (and thus) indicative of (his) sentiments, and scanned (him) with an eye turning round and round in affection, (and) laden with tears (of joy), (and) perceptive of (his noble) nature,-[to govern of a surety] the whole world;

(L. 9.) - Whose . . . some people (were accustomed to) taste with affection, displaying exceeding great joy when they beheld (his) many actions that resembled nothing of a mortal nature; (and) whose protection other people, afflicted by (his) prowess, sought, performing obeisance . . .

(L. 11.) - [Whose] . . .doers of great wrong, always conquered by his arm in battle . . . tomorrow and tomorrow . . .pride . . . repentance, with minds filled with contentment (and) expanding with much clearly displayed pleasure and affection. . . the spring (?). . .

(L. 13.) - By whom, having, unassisted, with the force of the prowess of (his) arm that rose up so as to pass all bounds, uprooted

Achyuta and Nāgasena . . . (by whom), causing him who was born in the family of the Kotas to be captured by (his) armies, (and) taking his pleasure at (the city) that had the name of Pushpa, while the sun . . . the banks . . .

(L. 15.) - (Of whom it used to be said) - "The building of the pale of religion; fame as white as the rays of the moon, (and) spreading far and wide; wisdom that pierced the essential nature of things; . . . calmness . . . ; the path of the sacred hymns, that is worthy to be studied; and even poetry, which gives free vent to the power of the mind of poets; (all these are his); (in short) what (virtue) is there that does not belong to him, who alone is a worthy subject of contemplation for those who can recognise merit and intellect ?"

(L. 17.) - Who was skilful in engaging in a hundred battles of various kinds;-whose only ally was the prowess of the strength of his own arm;-who was noted for prowess;-whose most charming body was covered over with all the beauty of the marks of a hundred confused wounds, caused by the blows of battle-axes, arrows, spears, pikes, barbed darts, swords, lances, javelins for throwing, iron arrows, vaitastikas, and many other (weapons). . .

(L. 19.) - Whose great good fortune was mixed with, so as to be increased by (his) glory produced by the favour shewn in capturing and then liberating Mahendra of Kosala, Vyāghrarāja of Mahākantāra, Mantarāja of Kerala, Mahendra of Pishṭapura, Svāmidatta of Koṭṭūra on the hill, Damana of Eranḍapalla, Vishnngopa of Kāñchi, Nīlarāja of Avamukta, Hastivarman of Vengī, Ugrasena of Palakka, Kubera of Devarāshṭra, Dhanaṃjaya of Kusthalapura, and all the other kings of the region of the south;-

(L. 21.) - Who abounded in majesty that had been increased by violently exterminating Rudradeva, Matila, Nāgadatta, Chandravarman, Ganapatināga, Nāgasena, Achyuta, Nandin, Balavarman, and many other kings of (the land of Āryāvarta;-who made all the kings of the forest countries to become (his) servants;

(L. 22.) - Whose imperious commands were fully gratified, by giving all (kinds of) taxes and obeying (his) orders and coming to perform obeisance, by the frontier-kings of Samataṭa, Ḍavāka, Kāmarūpa, Nepāla, Kartripura, and other (countries), and by the Mālavas, Ārjunāyanas, Yaudheyas, Mādrakas, Ābhīras, Prārjunas, Sanakānīkas, Kākas, Kharaparikas, and other (tribes);-

(L. 23.) - Whose tranquil fame, pervading the whole world, was generated by establishing (again) many royal families, fallen and deprived of sovereignty;-whose binding together of the (whole) world, by means of the amplitude of the vigour of (his) arm, was effected by the acts of respectful service, such as offering themselves as sacrifices, bringing presents of maidens, (giving) Garuḍa-tokens, (surrendering) the enjoyment of their own territories, soliciting (his) commands, &c., (rendered) by the Daivaputras, Shāhis, Shāhānushāhis, Śakas, and Muruṇḍas, and by the people of Siṃhala and all (other) dwellers in islands;-who had no antagonist (of equal power) in the world;-who, by the overflow of the multitude of (his) various virtues adorned by a hundred good actions, rubbed out the fame of other kings with the soles of (his) feet;-who, being incomprehensible, was the spirit that was the cause of the production of good and the destruction of evil;-who, being full of compassion, had a tender heart that could be won over simply by devotion and obeisance;-who was the giver of many hundreds of thousands of cows;-

(L. 26.) - Whose mind busied itself with the support and the initiation, &c., of the miserable, the poor, the helpless, and the afflicted;--who was the glorified personification of kindness to mankind;-who was equal to (the gods) Dhanada and Varuṇa and Indra and Antaka;-whose officers were always employed in restoring the wealth of the various kings who had been conquered by the strength of his arms....

(L. 27.) - Who put to shame (Kaśyapa) the preceptor of (Indra) the lord of the gods, and Tumburu, and Nārada, and others, by (his)

sharp and polished intellect and choral skill and musical accomplishments;- who established (his) title of 'king of poets' by various poetical compositions that were fit to be the means of subsistence of learned people;-whose many wonderful and noble deeds are worthy to be praised for a very long time....

(L. 28.) - Who was a mortal only in celebrating the rites of the observances of mankind, (but was otherwise) a god, dwelling on the earth;-who was the son of the son's son of the Mahārāja, the illustrious Gupta;- who was the son's son of the Mahārāja, the illustrious Ghatotkacha;--who was the son of the Mahārājādhirāja, the glorious Chandragupta (I.), (and)- the daughter's son of Lichchhavi, begotten on the Mahādevī Kumāradevī...

(L. 30.) - (And) chose fame,-ever heaped up higher and higher by the development of (his) liberality and prowess of arm and composure and (study of) the precepts of the scriptures,-travelling by many paths, purifies the three worlds, as if it were the pale yellow water of (the river) Gaṅgā, flowing quickly on being liberated from confinement in the thickets of the matted hair of (the god) Paśupati.

(L. 31.) - And this poetical composition,...(the work) of the Khādyaṭapākika, the son of the Mahādanḍanāyaka Dhruvabhūti, the Sāṃdhivigrahika and Kumārāmātya, the Mahādanḍanāyaka Harisheṇa, who is the slave of these same feet of the Bhattāraka, (and) whose mind is expanded by the favour of constantly walking about in (his) presence,-let it be for the welfare and happiness of all existing beings!

(L. 33.) - And the accomplishment of the matter has been effected by the Mahādanḍanāyaka Tilabhaṭṭaka, who meditates on the feet of the Paramabhaṭṭāraka.

This record gives the details of the extent of the biggest empire India had seen up to that point in time. In current history books, the Mauryan Empire is shown as being larger than the empire of the Imperial Guptas. This is based on the identification of

Devānāmpriya Priyadarśī with Aśoka Maurya and making the boundaries of the Mauryan Empire based on the locations of the inscriptions of Devānāmpriya Priyadarśī and the subjects mentioned in the inscriptions. As Kumāragupta-I was the real Devānāmpriya Priyadarśī, we now have an additional way of ascertaining the extent of Samudragupta's empire. We can take the empire of Devānāmpriya Priyadarśī and subtract from it the regions added by Chandragupta II, son of Samudragupta, and Kumāragupta-I, grandson of Samudragupta. Chandragupta II is not known to have added any significant region to his father's empire. He is credited with defeating the Sakas, but that is only to prove that he was the real Vikramāditya of the legends. There is no substance to it. He did not take the title Śakāri, enemy of the Śakas. So, the only significant addition to Samudragupta's empire was that of Kaliṅga, by Kumāragupta-I. Let's now see the extent of Samudragupta's empire, according to the Allahabad pillar inscription.

In line 19, a number of kings of South India are listed, who were captured and then liberated. These kings included Mahendra of (South) Kosala, Vyāghrarāja of Mahākantāra, Mantarāja of Kerala, Mahendra of Piṣṭapura, Svāmidatta of Koṭṭūra on the hill, Damana of Eranḍapalla, Viṣṇugopa of Kāñchi, Nīlarāja of Avamukta, Hastivarman of Vengī, Ugrasena of Palakka, Kubera of Devarāṣṭra, and Dhanaṃjaya of Kusthalapura. South Kośala was an ancient kingdom located in present day Chhatisgarh and Western Odisha. Kośala was the ancient kingdom, which was ruled by Ikṣvāku kings of Solar dynasty, in which Lord Rāma was born. Kośala was located in present day Uttar Pradesh with its capital at Ayodhya. After Lord Rāma's reign, his son Lava became the ruler of Kośala, and Rāma's second son Kuśa went south to establish the kingdom of Dakṣiṇa (South) Kośala with its capital at Kuśasthalipura. Mahākantāra was located in the present day Odisha. What has been translated as Kerala, by Fleet, is actually

Korala or Kurāla, and was located close to South Kośala [13]. Piṣṭapura is current day Pithapuram in Andhra Pradesh close to the east coast. Koṭṭūra was located in the vicinity of present day Ganjam district in Odisha [14]. Eranḍapalla was ancient Eranḍapali near current day Srikakulam (Chicacole) in Andhra Pradesh. Kāñchi is present day Kanchipuram in Tamil Nadu about 75 km from the capital Chennai. Location of Avamukta is uncertain. Vengī is present day Pedavegi in Andhra Pradesh. Palakka was located in the Nellore district of Andhra Pradesh and was a capital of the Pallavas [15]. Devarāṣṭra was located in the Vishakhapatnam district of Andhra Pradesh. Kusthalapura, which seems to be a variant of Kuśasthalipura, is currently unidentified. All these kingdoms were located on the eastern side of South India. What is conspicuous by its absence is the kingdom of Kaliṅga. This kingdom was so powerful that even the great conqueror Samudragupta did not dare to subdue it. His grandson Kumāragupta attacked Kaliṅga and conquered it, but the heavy price of the war resulted in great remorse and he converted to Buddhism as a result. Kumāragupta became a great patron of Buddhism and took the title of Devānāmpriya Priyadarśī.

In line 21, it is mentioned that a number of kings were violently exterminated, which included Rudradeva, Matila, Nāgadatta, Chandravarman, Gaṇapatināga, Nāgasena, Achyuta, Nandin, and Balavarman. Many of them were Nāga kings as is evident from the names Nāgadatta, Gaṇapatināga and Nāgasena. Based on literary and numismatic evidence, it can be said that Gaṇapatināga was the ruler of Mathura, Nāgasena of Padmāvatī, and Achyuta of Ahichchhatrā, current day Ramnagar village in Bareilly district of Uttar Pradesh [16]. King Nandin has not been identified by anyone yet and is usually tagged to Achyuta to make it king Achyutanandin. According to the Purāṇas, the last king of Vidisha was Bhūtinanda, as mentioned earlier in this chapter. We can identify Bhūtinanda as the king Nandin in Samudragupta's inscription. Chandrāṃśa was ruling when Alexander attacked India. He has been called Xandrames by the Greek historians. In the intervening years, between 326 BCE and 310 BCE, Chandrāṃśa was followed by Dhanadharman, who was followed by Vaṅgara. With the extermination of Nandin by Samudragupta, the Nāga rule in Vidisha came to an end. It was because of the rivalry with the Nāga kings that the Imperial Guptas chose Garuda (eagle) as their insignia as described in line 23. The eagle is the ruler of the skies, who is always watchful, has extraordinary vision, and pounces on the prey in one fast sweep with no chance of escape. The choice of the eagle as their insignia was befitting the might of the Imperial Guptas.

In line 22, Samudragupta gives a list of kingdoms that accepted his sovereignty without a fight. These kings paid taxes to him, obeyed his orders, and came to his court to pay obeisance. These kingdoms included Samataṭa, Ḍavāka, Kāmarūpa, Nepāla, Kartripura, as well as the kingdoms ruled by the Mālavas, Ārjunāyanas, Yaudheyas, Mādrakas, Ābhīras, Prārjunas, Sanakānīkas, Kākas, and Kharaparikas. Samataṭa means an area where rivers have flat and equal banks on both sides. This kingdom was located in present day Bangladesh and included the area around Noakhali, Barisal, Faridpur and Dhaka [17]. Ḍavāka is the area around the modern day town of Doboka and Kāmarūpa is the area around Kamrup district, both in Assam. Nepal still retains the old name Nepāla. Kartripura may have been in the region of Garhwal and Kumaon districts in Uttar Pradesh and Uttarakhand, which had a tradition of Kaṭūriā Rājpūtas [18]. Mālava had their capital at Ujjayinī, which was a centre for astronomy, and this is where the legends of Vikramāditya were conceived. Samudragupta was the first historical person to assume the title of Emperor Vikramāditya after Mālava people became his subjects. Ārjunāyanas ruled the territory formed by the Delhi-Jaipur-Agra triangle [19]. Yaudheya, as the name suggests, were a warlike people and earned a living by fighting, according to Pāṇini. Based on the find spots of their coins and coin moulds, they occupied parts of western Uttar Pradesh, Punjab and Haryana. The Madra kingdom was located between the Ravi and Chenab rivers with its capital at Śākala, present day Sialkot in Pakistan. According to the Mahābhārata, the king of Madra was Śalya. His sister Mādrī was the mother of the Pāṇḍava twins Nakula and Sahadeva, but Śalya was tricked into fighting on the side of the Kauravas. Ābhīra kingdom was located in the area of northern parts of Gujarat and southern parts of Rajasthan. Prārjuna, Sanakānīka, Kāka, and Kharaparika cannot be identified definitely. It can be said that they were at the south-western frontiers of Samudragupta's empire, as all other directions had been covered already.

In line 23, foreign rulers outside the empire of Samudragupta are listed. These rulers extended friendly overtures by offering presents. The list of such rulers includes Daivaputras, Shāhis, Shāhānushāhis, Śakas, and Murunḍas, and rulers of Siṃhala and other islands. Daivaputra means "son of God" and Alexander used to call himself "Son of Zeus", king of the gods in Greek mythology. Alexander's successors continued to espouse this belief and thus Greek rulers are the Daivaputra. The reference to giving their daughter in marriage (Kanyopāyanadāna) refers to Seleucus giving his daughter in marriage to Samudragupta. This again confirms that Seleucus had given his daughter in marriage to Samudragupta, and not to his father Chandragupta-I. The Shāhis, Shāhānushāhis and Śaka Murunḍa refer to rulers from Persia or of Persian descent. Śaka Murunḍa may simply mean king of the Śakas [20]. We also have evidence of the growing naval power of the Imperial Guptas under Samudragupta by the reference to the rulers of Siṃhala (Sri Lanka) and other islands paying obeisance to him.

In line 14, Samudragupta says that he enjoyed himself in the city named Puṣpa (flower). This city named Puṣpapura or Kusumapura had a more familiar name, Kānyakubja, and was destined to play a much greater role in the affairs of India from the time of Samudragupta. As the Imperial Guptas expanded their empire, they had to shift their base from Pāṭaliputra to effectively govern the empire. The Imperial Gupta capital was first moved from Pāṭaliputra to Prayāga (Allahabad). This is the reason that Samudragupta's pillar is located in Prayāga. It was always there. It was not brought there from Kauśāmbī. The Prayāga pillar was not erected by Aśoka, but by Samudragupta as a symbol of his glory. What are considered the inscriptions of Aśoka are in fact inscriptions of Kumāragupta-I, grandson of Samudragupta. As the Imperial Gupta Empire expanded further to include parts of current day Afghanistan, the capital was moved further west to Kānyakubja, current day Kannauj in Farrukhabad district in Uttar Pradesh. Kānyakubja attained great fame and prosperity during the rule of the Imperial Guptas and was considered the de-facto capital of India since then till the time of Jaichand towards the close of the 12th century. The rivalry between Prithviraj Chauhan and Jaichand was not just about the marriage of Jaichand's daughter Sanyuktā with Prithviraj Chauhan without her father's approval, but about both of them having the haughty feeling of being the de facto ruler of India. Jaichand considered himself the ruler of India as he governed from Kānyakubja, while Prithviraj Chauhan considered himself the ruler of India as he ruled from Delhi, where Indraprastha, the seat of power during the time of the Mahābhārata, was located. Kānyakubja was a city famous for the manufacture of perfume from flowers and was called Kusumapura or Puṣpapura for this reason. There is an interesting story about how Kānyakubja got its name. We get the following account of the naming of Kānyakubja from Xuan Zang (Hiuen Tsiang) [21]:

> *"The old capital of Kanyakubja, where men lived for a long time, was called Kusumapura. The king's name was Brahmadatta. His religious merit and wisdom in former births entailed on him the*

inheritance of a literary and military character that caused his name to be widely reverenced and feared. The whole of Jambudvipa resounded with his fame, and the neighbouring provinces were filled with the knowledge of it. He had 1000 sons famed for wisdom and courage, and 100 daughters of singular grace and beauty.

At this time there was a Rishi living on the border of the Ganges river, who, having entered a condition of ecstasy, by his spiritual power passed several myriad of years in this condition, until his form became like a decayed tree. Now it happened that some wandering birds having assembled in a flock near this spot, one of them let drop on the shoulder (of the Rishi) a Nyagrodha (Ni-ku-liu) fruit, which grew up, and through summer and winter afforded him a welcome protection and shade. After a succession of years he awoke from his ecstasy. He arose and desired to get rid of the tree, but feared to injure the nests of the birds in it. The men of the time, extolling his virtue, called him "The great-tree (Mahavriksha) Rishi." The Rishi gazing once on the river-bank as he wandered forth to behold the woods and trees, saw the daughters of the king following one another and gambolling together. Then the love of the world (the world of desire-Kamadhatu), which holds and pollutes the mind, was engendered in him. Immediately he went to Kusumapura for the purpose of paying his salutations to the king and asking (for his daughter).

The king, hearing of the arrival of the Rishi went himself to meet and salute him, and thus addressed him graciously: "Great Rishi! you were reposing in peace-what has disturbed you?" The Rishi answered, "After having reposed in the forest many years, on awaking from my trance, in walking to and fro I saw the king's daughters a polluted and lustful heart was produced in me, and now I have come from far to request (one of your daughters in marriage)."

The king hearing this, and seeing no way to escape, said to the Rishi, "Go back to your place and rest, and let me beg you to await the happy period." The Rishi, hearing the mandate, returned to the forest. The king then asked his daughters in succession, but none of them consented to be given in marriage.

The king, fearing the power of the Rishi, was much grieved and afflicted thereat. And now the youngest daughter of the king, watching an opportunity when the king was at liberty, with an engaging manner said, "The king my father, has his thousand sons, and on every side his dependents are reverently obedient. Why, then, are you sad as if you were afraid of something?"

The king replied, "The great-tree-Rishi has been pleased to look down on you to seek a marriage with one of you, and you have all turned away and not consented to comply with his request. Now this Rishi possesses great power, and is able to bring either calamities or good fortune. If he is thwarted he will be exceedingly angry, and in his displeasure destroy my kingdom, and put an end to our religious worship, and bring disgrace on me and my ancestors. As I consider this unhappiness indeed I have much anxiety."

The girl-daughter replied, "Dismiss your heavy grief; ours is the fault. Let me, I pray, in my poor person promote the prosperity of the country."

The king hearing her words, was overjoyed, and ordered his chariot to accompany her with gifts to her marriage. Having arrived at the hermitage of the Rishi, he offered his respectful greetings and said, "Great Rishi! since you condescended to fix your mind on external things and to regard the world with complacency, I venture to offer you my young daughter to cherish and provide for you (water and sweep)." The Rishi, looking at her, was displeased, and said to the king, "You despise my old age, surely, in offering me this ungainly thing."

The king said, "I asked all my daughters in succession, but they were unwilling to comply with your request: this little one alone offered to serve you."

> *The Rishi was extremely angry, and uttered this curse (evil charm), saying, "Let the ninety-nine girls (who refused me) this moment become hump-backed; being thus deformed, they will find no one to marry them in all the world." The king, having sent a messenger in haste, found that already they had become deformed. From this time the town had this other name of the Kuih-niu-shing (Kanyakubja), i.e., city of the humped-backed women."*

As discussed above, Kānyakubja became the de-facto capital of India since the time of Samudragupta. It was from here that Harṣavardhana ruled. Still later, a tripartite struggle followed between Rāṣṭrakūta, Pāla and Pratihāra rulers for the control of Kānyakubja. With his capital at Kānyakubja, Samudragupta ruled his vast empire for a long time. Samudragupta was a great Hindu emperor, who embodied all the good qualities of the legendary king Vikramāditya. He was full of compassion, had a tender heart, and was a great benefactor of the poor and the helpless. He was kindness personified. He was not only a great warrior, but also possessed a sharp and polished intellect. He was an accomplished musician and a poet of note.

Samudragupta was the first emperor to take the title of Vikramāditya. It is proven from the fact that on one of his coins his title is given as Śrī Vikrama [22]. Samudragupta also took the title of Parākramāṅka, which is shown on his coins. Parākramāṅka, which means that valour was his characteristic mark, is synonymous to Sāhasāṅka, which means that courage was his characteristic mark. In Abhijñāna Śākuntalam, Vikramāditya has been called Sāhasāṅka by Kālidāsa and in the Mahoba Fort inscription, the era has been specified as belonging to Sāhasāṅka, which modern historians take as the Vikrama era [23]. Kṣiraswāmī, a commentator on Amarakoṣa, has equated Sāhasāṅka with Vikramāditya, and the same has been done by Ratna Miśra in his commentary of Saraswatīkaṇṭhābharaṇa [24]. Having shown that Samudragupta had taken the title of Vikramāditya, it is now time to go over one of the literary references to Vikramāditya that has its origin in the generosity of Samudragupta.

King Hāla Sātavāhana, who is currently dated in the first century CE, has given the example of emperor Vikramāditya's generosity in a verse in Gāthāsaptaśatī. This is fatal to currently accepted chronology, as it does not accept any Vikramāditya in the first century BCE and the Imperial Gupta emperor it credits with being Vikramāditya is placed in the fourth century CE. As always, interpolation is invoked to rescue modern chronology. The concerned verse in Prākṛta is reproduced below [25]:

> *"Saṃvāhaṇasuharasatosieṇa daṃteṇa tuha kare lakkham.*
> *Chalaṇeṇa vikkamaichcha chariam anusikkhiam tissā."*

This verse can be translated in Sanskrit as follows:

> *"saṃvāhana sukharasatoṣitena dattena tava kare lākṣām.*
> *charaṇeṇa vikramādityacharitram anusikṣitam tasyāḥ."*

The background of this verse can be described as such:

A husband or lover was massaging the feet of his beloved. Her feet were red because of the application of the paste of a red die called lakkha in Prākṛta or lākṣā inSanskrit. Because of this, the husband or lover's hands also became red. The poet then says:

> *"The feet of your beloved being satisfied by the massage have given lakkha (red die) in your hands. In doing this (giving lakkha or one hundred thousand) they have followed the character of Vikramāditya."*

We should note that lakkha has been used as having two meanings here. The generosity of Samudragupta has been described in the Allahabad pillar inscription, in which he has claimed to have given a hundred thousand cows in gift. This poem refers to this incidence of generosity by Samudragupta Vikramāditya.

Samudragupta was a very able administrator, and opted for different policies for different kingdoms. Some of them, like the

Nāgas, were exterminated and their kingdoms were made part of the empire, while others, such as Vākāṭakas, were allowed to rule as long as they were subordinate to him.

4.5 The Vākāṭakas

The Vākāṭakas were a powerful force in the south, and as long as they were united and their alliance with the Nāgas was intact, the Imperial Guptas were not in a position to subdue them. The founder of the Vākāṭaka dynasty was Vindhyaśakti. Literary and epigraphic data suggest that Vindhyaśakti was ruling from the region of Vidarbha in Maharashtra. The Vākāṭakas rapidly rose in power under the rule of Pravarasena-I, son of Vindhyaśakti. He performed a number of Vedic sacrifices and assumed the title of Samrāṭa -- a term used in ancient India to signify a universal monarch. Pravarasena-I cemented an alliance with the powerful Nāga king Bhavanāga by getting his son Gautamiputra married to the daughter of Bhavanāga in circa 330 BCE. Gautamiputra predeceased his father. Pravarasena-I ruled for sixty years and after his death in 310 BCE, there was a battle for succession. The Vākāṭaka empire broke apart and Rudrasena-I, grandson of Pravarasena-I, ascended the throne of the main branch, while Sarvasena, second son of Pravarasena-I, founded the Vatsagulma branch. Pravarasena-I had four sons, and the other two sons may have held parts of the Vākāṭaka Empire. At this time, the unity of Nāga alliance also fell apart, as they took sides in the family feud of the Vākāṭakas. This provided the opportunity to the Imperial Guptas to quickly sweep upon the unsuspecting Nāgas and carry on with the mission of establishing a mighty empire, the like of which India had not seen before. As Chandragupta-I and Samudragupta continued on their victorious march, the divided Vākāṭakas were in no position to engage in a direct fight with the Imperial Guptas and simply accepted their sovereignty. It is for this reason that no Vākāṭaka king after Pravarasena-I assumed the title of Samrāṭa. Rudrasena-I was succeeded by his son Prithvīsena-I, who was succeeded by his son Rudrasena II. Rudrasena II was married to Prabhāvatīguptā, daughter of Imperial Gupta emperor Chandragupta II, who himself was married to Kuberanāgā, a Nāga princess. Thus, once sovereignty of the Imperial Guptas was established over the Vākāṭakas and the Nāgas, friendly relations followed by the consummation of marriage alliances between them. With the foregoing in mind, the revised chronology of the Imperial Guptas and the Vākāṭakas is shown in Tables 4.1 and 4.2.

Table 4.1: New Chronology of Imperial Guptas

Gupta Monarch	**Regnal years**	**Current Timeline [26]**	**Proposed Timeline**
Chandragupta I	1-31	319-50 CE	309-294 BCE
Samudragupta	31-57	350-76 CE	294-252 BCE
Chandragupta II	57-96	376-415 CE	252-213 BCE
Kumāragupta I	96-128	415-447 CE	213-173 BCE
Ghatotkachagupta	129-136	448-455 CE	
Skandagupta	137-148	456-467 CE	172-161 BCE
Narasiṃhagupta	148-155	467-474 CE	161-154 BCE
Kumāragupta II	155-157	474-476 CE	154-152 BCE
Budhagupta	158-169	477-488 CE	151-140 BCE
Vainyagupta II	189	506 CE	120 BCE
Viṣṇugupta	196	515 CE	113 BCE

The data on regnal years in Table 4.1 has been calculated from the dynastic chart given in the paper "Later Gupta History: Inscriptions, Coins and Historical Ideology" by Michael Willis [26]. Using these regnal years with the start date of 309 BCE for Imperial Gupta era will imply that Chandragupta I ruled from 309-278 BCE and Samudragupta ruled from 278-252 BCE.

Table 4.2: New Chronology of Vākāṭakas

Vākāṭaka King	**Accepted Date [27]**	**Proposed Date**
Vindhyaśakti I	250 CE	390 BCE
Pravarasena I	270 CE	370 BCE
Main branch		
Rudrasena I	330 CE	310 BCE
Prithvīsena I	350 CE	290 BCE
Rudrasena II	400 CE	240 BCE
Divākarasena	405 CE	235 BCE
Pravarasena II	420 CE	220 BCE
Narendrasena	450 CE	190 BCE
Prithvīsena II	470 CE	170 BCE
Vatsagulma branch		
Sarvasena	330 CE	310 BCE
Vindhyaśakti II	355 CE	285 BCE
Pravarasena II	400 CE	240 BCE
Son (unnamed)	410 CE	240 BCE
Devasena	450 CE	190 BCE
Harisena	475 CE	165 BCE
Son (unnamed)	500 CE	140 BCE

Assuming Chandragupta-I to be 20-years-old when he married Kumāradevī in 330 BCE, Chandragupta-I would be 41-years-old when he ascended the throne in 309 BCE. This seems fine and appropriate for his age. The problem is with the duration of his reign. If Chandragupta-I ruled for 31 years till 278 BCE, he would be 72-years-old at that time, and assuming Samudragupta to have been born in 329 BCE, he would be 51-years-old when he ascended the throne. This would be too late for a conqueror like Samudragupta, who claims in the Allahabad pillar inscription that his father gave him the throne saying that he was worthy while his eyes were filled with the tears of joy. Obviously, Chandragupta-I did not wait for old age to coronate Samudragupta. There is no record of Chandragupta-I ruling for 31 years. The first record of the Imperial Gupta regnal years is provided by Chandragupta-I, who said that it was his fifth year of reign when the Imperial Gupta year was 61. Thus we are justified in assuming that Chandragupta-I ruled for about 15 years and then placed Samudragupta on throne in 294 BCE. Thus, Chandragupta-I was about 56 years old when he abdicated the throne and Samudragupta was about 35-years-old when he ascended the throne. Rest of the revised chronology of the Imperial Guptas in Table 4.1 is derived by counting the regnal years from 309 BCE.

A revised chronology of the Vākāṭakas is shown in Table 4.2 based on the data for currently accepted chronology from "Inscriptions of the Vākāṭakas" edited by Mirashi [27]. The revised chronology is derived based on the assumption that Pravarasena-I died in 310 BCE and then calculating backward and forward using the regnal years provided by the accepted chronology.

Assuming that Samudragupta got married to the daughter of Seleucus-I Nicator in 303 BCE, it is possible that Chandragupta II was born around 290 BC, as he had an elder brother named Ramagupta. Samudragupta might have been busy with his military campaigns as well. This would make Chandragupta II about 38-years-old in 252 BCE, when he ascended the throne. The marriage of his daughter Prabhāvatīguptā to the Vākāṭaka crown prince Rudrasena II could have taken place in 245 BCE, when

Chandragupta II was about 45–years-old and Prabhāvatīguptā was of a marriageable age. Kuberanāgā, mother of Prabhāvatīguptā, has been called Mahādevī in the Poona copper plate of Prabhāvatīguptā issued in the 13th year, but has been called only Devī in the Riddhapur plates of Pravarasena II issued in the 19th year [28]. This is probably related to the elevation of Dhruvadevī to the position of Mahādevī by Chandragupta II. In the Imperial Gupta inscriptions of the successors of Chandragupta II, Dhruvadevī has been called Mahādevī. So Kuberanāgā was already married to Chandragupta II and became the Mahādevī when Chandragupta II killed his brother Ramagupta and ascended the throne. Later, this position was accorded to Dhruvadevī, after Chandragupta II married her. Chandragupta II had to wait a while to marry Dhruvadevī to avoid public censure.

4.6 Chandragupta II Vikramāditya

After Samudragupta, his son Chandragupta II ascended the throne, who officially took the title of Vikramāditya. Modern historians have made Chandragupta II as the Vikramāditya of the legends and placed Kālidāsa in his court. According to Indian tradition, Kālidāsa was in the court of Vikramāditya, who died in 57 BCE. Chandragupta II Vikramāditya ruled in the fourth century CE according to modern historians, and third century BCE according to the chronology developed in this book. Either way, he cannot be the Vikramāditya in whose memory the Vikrama era was instituted, and whose court was adorned by Kālidāsa and rest of the nine gems. In fact, Chandragupta II Vikramāditya is the weakest Vikramāditya among the four historical Vikramādityas who have added to the legends of Vikramāditya. His only claim to fame in the current version of history is the defeat of Śakas for which there is no direct evidence. This has been done to prove that he was the Śakāri (enemy of the Śakas) Vikramāditya. Numismatic evidence is presented in support of this thesis, but this evidence is at best circumstantial. There are some stories about Vikramāditya that fit Chandragupta II, and we will present them now.

The source of the first story is the book Devīchandragupta written by Viśākhadatta. This book is not available now, but has been referenced or quoted in many later books such as the commentary on Bharata's Nāṭyaśāstra composed by Abhinavagupta, Śṛṅgāraprakāśa composed by Bhoja, Nāṭyadarpaṇa composed by Rāmachandra and Guṇachandra, and Nāṭakalaksanaratnakosa composed by Sāgaranandin [29].

According to this story, there was a king named Rāmagupta, who was hopelessly cornered by the Śakas during a war. He agreed to surrender his queen Dhruvadevī to the Śakas to secure his release. His younger brother Kumāra Chandragupta balked at this idea and instead offered to go to the enemy camp dressed as the queen and kill the Śaka king. He succeeded in his plan and saved the honour of the family. He became a hero not only for the public but the queen also, while the reputation of Rāmagupta suffered badly. Fearing for his life, Chandragupta feigned madness and killed Rāmagupta at an opportune time. Chandragupta then became the king and married Dhruvadevī.

References to this story have been made in several inscriptions by Rāṣṭrakūṭa rulers [30], which mean that this story was considered to be historical when these inscriptions were made. In the Sanjana plates, Rāṣṭrakūṭa emperor Amoghavarṣa claims superiority over a Gupta king who had killed his brother and seized the throne and the queen. In the Cambay and Sangli plates, Rāṣṭrakūṭa emperor Govinda IV claims to be as daring as Sāhasāṅka, but his reputation was not sullied by a sexual union with his brother's wife, and he did not treat his elder brother cruelly even though he could have done so if he wanted to.

This story is also found in a Muslim chronicle called Majmal-ul-Tawārīkh [31]. There was a king named Rawwāl, who had a brother named Barkamarīs. A princess had chosen Barkamarīs to be her husband, but Rawwāl got married to her. Sometime later, Rawwāl was attacked by an enemy and found refuge in a fort along with his nobles. The enemy king asked him to send his wife with a girl from each noble to get a safe passage. Rawwāl was ready to accept the proposal, but Barkamarīs proposed another plan. He dressed as the queen and killed the enemy, while the sons of other officers dressed as maids killed other officers of the enemy. A minister incited Rawwāl against Barkamarīs, who feigned madness to save himself and killed Rawwāl at an opportune time. Barkamarīs then became the king and married the widowed queen. It is obvious that in this story Rawwāl represents Rāmagupta, and Barkamarīs represents Vikramāditya.

We have another story about Vikramāditya that fits Chandragupta II, which is as follows [32]:

> *"To the south of Vasubandhu's house, about fifty paces or so, is a second storied-pavilion in which Manorhita, a master of Śāstras, composed the Vibhāsha Śāstra. This learned doctor flourished in the midst of the thousand years after the Nirvāṇa of Buddha. In his youth he was devoted to study and had distinguished talent. His fame was wide spread with the religious, and laymen sought to do him hearty reverence. At that time Vikramāditya, king of the country of Śrāvastī, was of wide renown. He ordered his ministers to distribute daily throughout India five lakhs of gold coin; he largely (everywhere) supplied the wants of the poor, the orphan, and the bereaved. His treasurer, fearing that the resources of the kingdom would be exhausted, represented the case to the king, and said, "Mahārāja! your fame has reached to the very lowest of your subjects, and extends to the brute creation. You bid me add (to your expenditure) five lakhs of gold to succour the poor throughout the world. Your treasury will thus be emptied, and then fresh imposts will have to be laid (on the land cultivators), until the resources of the land be also exhausted; then the voice of complaint will be heard*

and hostility be provoked. Your majesty, indeed, will get credit for charity, but your minister will lose the respect of all." The king answered, "But of my own surplus I (wish to) relieve the poor. I would on no account, for my own advantage, thoughtlessly burthen (grind down) the country." Accordingly he added five lakhs for the good of the poor. Some time after this the king was engaged chasing a boar. Having lost the track, he gave a man a lakh for putting him on the scent again. Now Manorhita, the doctor of Śāstras, once engaged a man to shave his head, and gave him offhand a lakh of gold for so doing. This munificent act was recorded in the annals by the chief historian. The king reading of it was filled with shame, and his proud heart continually fretted about it, and so he desired to bring some fault against Manorhita and punish him. So he summoned an assembly of different religious persons whose talents were most noted, to the number of one hundred, and issued the following decree: "I wish to put a check to the various opinions (wanderings) and to settle the true limits (of inquiry); the opinions of different religious sects are so various that the mind knows not what to believe. Exert your utmost ability, therefore, to-day in following out my directions." On meeting for discussion he made a second decree: "The doctors of law belonging to the heretics are distinguished for their ability. The Shamans and the followers of the law (of Buddha) ought to look well to the principles of their sect; if they prevail, then they will bring reverence to the law of Buddha; but if they fail, then they shall be exterminated." On this, Manorhita questioned the heretics and silenced ninety-nine of them. And now a man was placed (sat on the mat to dispute with him) of no ability whatever, and for the sake of a trifling discussion (Manorhita) proposed the subject of fire and smoke. On this the king and the heretics cried out saying, "Manorhita, the doctor of Śāstras, has lost the sense of right connection (mistaken the order or sense of the phrase); he should have named smoke first and fire afterwards: this order of things is constant." Manorhita wishing to explain the difficulty, was not allowed a hearing; on which, ashamed to see himself thus treated by the people, he bit out his tongue and wrote a

> *warning to his disciple Vasubandhu, saying, "In the multitude of partisans there is no justice; among persons deceived there is no discernment." Having written this, he died.*
>
> *A little afterwards Vikramāditya-rājā lost his kingdom and was succeeded by a monarch who widely patronised those distinguished for literary merit. Vasubandhu, wishing to wash out the former disgrace, came to the king and said, "Mahārājā, by your sacred qualities you rule the empire and govern with wisdom. My old master, Manorhita, was deeply versed in the mysterious doctrine. The former king, from an old resentment, deprived him of his high renown. I now wish to avenge the injury done to my master." The king, knowing that Manorhita was a man of superior intelligence approved of the noble project of Vasubandhu; he summoned the heretics who had discussed with Manorhita. Vasubandhu having exhibited afresh the former conclusions of his master, the heretics were abashed and retired."*

Before we try to identify the Vikramāditya with whom this story is associated and thereby find a date for Vasubandhu, we should note a few points. Vikramāditya is a hero, and a paragon of virtues in all of Hindu and Jain literature. When we come to Buddhist literature, however, we see them writing unsavoury things about him. Clearly, the Buddhists were playing the game of one-upmanship, seeking to showcase their faith as superior to the rest. Not only that, they declared the people who were not following the path laid out by the Buddha were heretics.

Keeping these points in mind, it becomes clear that the Vikramāditya vilified in this Buddhist legend was Chandragupta II. Since Manorhita lost the debate, Buddhists claimed that the debate was rigged, and made a story about it. From where was a Buddhist monk Manorhit supposed to get one hundred thousand gold coins to give to a barber? Since Manorhit's disciple Vasubandhu won the debate against the heretics under the new king, the new king must have been favorable to Buddhists, and therefore likely a Buddhist himself. This fits well with Chandragupta II Vikramāditya and his son Kumāragupta-I Mahendrātitya, who had become a Buddhist and taken the title of Devānāmpriya Priyadarśī. As Kumāragupta-I ruled towards the end of third century BCE, this is the time of Vasubandhu. This is also consistent with our dating of the Buddha in 13th century BCE as the time of Vasubandhu was 1000 years after the Buddha, according to the text quoted above. Some historians are of the opinion that the Vikramāditya of this story was Skandagupta, but he does not measure up to the level of generosity that Vikramāditya displays in this story. Skandagupta's empire was under siege from the beginning of his coronation and he could not have afforded this kind of munificence. The reason Skandagupta found himself under such dire circumstances was not his fault at all. It was in response to the messages of peace that his father Kumaragupta-I was relaying all over his empire and beyond. Little did Kumaragupta-I realize that his messages of peace would be taken as signs of weakness and barbarians would consider it as an open invitation to invade.

Notes

1. Mahābhārata 1.3.20.
2. Fleet (1888): 241.
3. Pargiter (1913): 72-73.
4. Mookerji (1973): 19.
5. Mirashi (1974): 33.
6. Bakshi and Ralhan (2007): 103.
7. McCrindle (1893): 327-328.
8. McCrindle (1893): 310-311.
9. McCrindle (1893): 310.
10. McCrindle (1901): 88-89.
11. Fleet (1888): 20-21.

12. Fleet (1888): 10-17.
13. Agrawal (1989): 108.
14. Agrawal (1989): 109.
15. Goyala (1987b): 187.
16. Goyala (1987b): 196-197.
17. Agrawal (1989): 118.
18. Agrawal (1989): 118.
19. Agrawal (1989): 119.
20. Agrawal (1989): 123.
21. Beal (1906): 207-209.
22. Goyala (1987b): 67.
23. Pandey (1951): 89.
24. Nirmala (1992): 125
25. Vyāsa (1990): 94.
26. Willis (2005).
27. Mirashi (1963): vi.
28. Jain (1972): 232.
29. Sircar (1969): 138.
30. Sircar (1969): 141.
31. Sircar (1969): 143-145.
32. Beal (1906): 105-109.

"Let us recollect that peace or war will not always be left to our option; that however moderate or unambitious we may be, we cannot count upon the moderation, or hope to extinguish the ambition of others."

- Alexander Hamilton

5. PEACE HAS NO TAKERS

The Great Seal of the Unites States has a picture in the centre of a bald eagle with its wings stretched. The eagle holds a bundle of 13 arrows in the left talon and an olive branch in the right talon. The eagle's head is turned right looking at the olive branch. The eagle as the bird of prey ruling the skies is the symbol of the might of the United States. The bundle of 13 arrows representing the 13 original states symbolizes the battle ready status of the Unites States to defend its interests. The olive branch represents peace. The eagle looking at the olive branch represents the preference for peace. The Great Seal of the Unites States sends the powerful message that the Unites States desires peace, but will not hesitate to go to war to protect its interests.

Peace does not come for free. There is always a price to be paid for peace. There are times when the price of peace is far greater than the price of war. Peace can only be negotiated from a position of strength. When we let our guard down the barbarians come invading. This was exactly what happened when Kumāragupta-I became the messenger of peace.

5.1 Beloved of the Gods

Kumāragupta-I ascended the throne in 213 BCE and ruled for 40 years till 173 BCE. Supposing he was about 75 years old when he died or abandoned the throne, he would have been 35-years-old when he ascended the throne. This means that he was born around 248 BCE. In the last chapter, we had estimated that Chandragupta II was born around 290 BCE, and so he was about 42-years-old when Kumāragupta-I was born. This seems reasonable considering that Kumāragupta's mother was Dhruvadevī, who was not the first wife of Chandragupta II. Kuberanāgā was the first wife of Chandragupta II. Chandragupta II married Dhruvadevī after killing his brother Ramagupta and had to wait a while to marry Dhruvadevī to avoid public criticism.

The most important event of Kumāragupta's life was his attack on Kaliṅga. As this attack took place during the eighth year of his rule, Kaliṅga was attacked in 206 BCE. Kaliṅga was so powerful and its people were such fierce warriors that even Samudragupta had not tried to subjugate them. Chandragupta II, who had assumed the title of Vikramāditya, also thought it wise to leave Kaliṅga alone. Kumāragupta tried to subjugate Kaliṅga, the final frontier, but found out that the cost of this war was far beyond what he had anticipated. Kumāragupta managed to win the war, but the magnitude of the loss of lives in the battlefield and the sorrows of people affected by the war transformed him. In the aftermath of this war, a repentant Kumāragupta became a Buddhist. He assumed the title of Devānāmpriya Priyadarśī and started to spread Buddhism earnestly.

Around the same time, as Kumāragupta was busy planning for the Kaliṅga war or was already engaged in the war, Greek king Antiochus III Megas, who was distantly related to Kumāragupta, came to the western frontier of India. Kumāragupta's grandmother, wife of Samudragupta, was the daughter of Seleucus-I Nicator. Antiochus III Megas was the son of Seleucus II Callinicus, who was the son of Antiochus II Theos. Antiochus II Theos was the son of Antiochus-I Soter, who was the son of Seleucus-I Nicator. Thus grandmother of Kumāragupta was the sister of the great grandfather of Antiochus III Megas. Since Kumāragupta was busy with the Kaliṅga war preparation on the eastern frontier of his empire, it was Sophagasenas, the viceroy of Kumāragupta, who met Antiochus III on his behalf. Antiochus III returned after receiving gifts from Sophagasenus, which included some war elephants.

The greatest contribution of Kumāragupta-I was the establishment of Nālandā University, which became a premier institute of learning. As Kumāragupta-I was the real Devānāmpriya Priyadarśī and Aśoka the Great has been granted greatness because of his erroneous identification with Devānāmpriya Priyadarśī, historians have to decide now whether Kumāragupta-I should be called Kumāragupta-I the Great.

A realistic assessment of Devānāmpriya Priyadarśī has been made by Professor Basham [1], which is that of a naïve and credulous person. In the first minor rock edict Devānāmpriya Priyadarśī claims that gods were freely mixing with men due to his strenuous faith-related activities. In the fourth rock edict he speaks of the appearance of divine chariots and balls of fire. These edicts show that Buddhists were indulging in cheap propaganda for the propagation of their faith and Kumāragupta-I was credulous enough to believe them. Here is clear proof that the use of fake miracles to convert people was started long ago by Buddhists. As it turns out others have also learnt this trick. In the 13th Rock Edict he claims that he had gained victory of Dhamma on all his frontiers as far away as the realms of Antiochus, Ptolemy, Antigonus, Magas and Alexander. However, Greek sources are totally silent about him. The effect, if at all any, was so small that it did not come to the notice of any Greek author. In the Kandahar edicts he claims that all the fishermen have stopped fishing and all the hunters have stopped hunting. This is simply impossible and no doubt he was being fed this kind of information by sycophants. This goes on to show how naïve and credulous he had become. It is a typical mindset of individuals brainwashed by religion. They lose touch with reality and start living in the make-believe world created by their own religious fantasies. While Kumāragupta-I lost touch with reality and continued to believe that his propagation of Dhamma had created a peaceful world all around, the empire was crumbling from within and barbarians were pounding at the gates. It fell upon his son Skandagupta to fight the rebellion and deter the barbarians, the acts of bravery that justified his title as Vikramāditya.

5.2 Skandagupta Vikramāditya

After Kumāragupta, his son Skandagupta ascended the throne and ruled for 12 years from 172-161 BCE. The next Imperial Gupta ruler after Skandagupta was Narasiṃhagupta, but he did not include Skandagupta in the genealogy. Narasiṃhagupta lists Purugupta as his father and son of Kumāragupta. It stands to reason that Skandagupta was the step-brother of Purugupta, as Skandagupta does not name his mother in his inscriptions. We now know that Skandagupta assumed the title of Vikramāditya. We also know that Purugupta, a supposedly elder brother of Skandagupta, did not rule or ruled for a very short time. This immediately brings to mind the story of Bhartṛhari and Vikramāditya.

The story about Bhartṛhari is told in Siṃhāsana-dwātṛṃśikā (popularly known as Siṃhāsana Battīsī). There was a king called Bhartṛhari, who ruled over Ujjayinī. He had a very beautiful wife named Anaṅgasenā. King Bhartṛhari had a younger brother named Vikramāditya. A poor Brāhmaṇa received a fruit from a Goddess after propitiating her and was told by the Goddess that whoever ate that fruit would become immortal. The Brāhmaṇa gifted the fruit to king Bhartṛhari. King Bhartṛhari loved his wife dearly, so he gifted the fruit to her. The queen was in love with a servant and gave the fruit to him, who in turn gave it to a servant maid. She loved a cowherd and gave the fruit to him, who in turn gave it to a girl who carried cow dung. The girl collected the cattle droppings in a basket and put the basket on her head and placed the fruit on top of the cattle droppings. When she was walking on the road, king Bhartṛhari saw the fruit on her head. After investigation, he found the truth and was very depressed. He retired to a forest after renouncing the world. Vikramāditya became the king of Ujjayinī after Bhartṛhari renounced the throne.

This story brings us to a tantalizing prospect that Purugupta was king Bhartṛhari. We also have an interesting connection in this regard. This connection is a place called Bhitari in Uttar Pradesh, about 15 km east of the confluence of the Gomati and the Ganges rivers. Here is what Captain Wilford had to say about this place [2]:

> *"Bhartrihari, according to the Hindus in general, withdrew to Chunār near Benares, where he remained some time; when his brother gave him a purganah, or small district, called to this day Bhartari, and Bhittri, after him; and which is to the eastward of the mouth of the river Gomti. There are the remains of a pretty large fort, with the ruins of his palace."*

So, we learn that Bhitari is a corrupt form of Bhartṛhari. We also know that Skandagupta had an inscription written on a pillar in Bhitari. This cannot be sheer coincidence. We can surmise that Bhartṛhari made his abode at Bhitari after Skandagupta provided the facility to him. As his son Narasiṃhagupta was a minor at this time, Skandagupta took over the reigns of the Imperial Gupta Empire. He had many challenges to face right from the beginning, which he has described in the Bhitari pillar inscription as follows [3]:

"[Perfection has been attained]! The son of the Mahārājādhirāja, the glorious Samudragupta,-who was the exterminator of all kings; who had no antagonist (of equal power) in the world; whose fame was tasted by the waters of the four oceans; who was equal to (the gods) Dhanada and Varuṇa and Indra and Antaka; who was the very axe of (the god) Kṛtānta; who was the giver of many millions of lawfully acquired cows and gold; who was the restorer of the aśvamedha-sacrifice, that had been long in abeyance; who was the son of the son's son of the Mahārāja, the illustrious Gupta; who was the son's son of the Mahārāja, the illustrious Ghatotkacha; (and) who was the son of the Mahārājādhirāja, the glorious Chandragupta (I.), (and) the daughter's son of Lichchhivi, begotten on the Mahādevī Kumrādevī,-

(L. 4.) - (was) the most devout worshipper of the Divine One, the Mahārājādhirāja, the glorious Chandragupta (II.), who was accepted by him; who was begotten on the Mahādevī Dattadevī; (and) who was himself without an antagonist (of equal power).

(L.5.) - His son (was) the most devout worshipper of the Divine One, the Mahārājādhirāja, the glorious Kumāragupta, who meditated on his feet, (and) who was begotten on the Mahādevī Dhruvadevī.

(L. 6.) - The son of him, the king, who was renowned for the innate power of (his) mighty intellect (and) whose fame was great, (is) this (present) king, by name Skandagupta, who possesses great glory; who subsisted (like a bee) on the wide-spreading waterlilies which were the feet of (his) father; whose fame is spread far and wide; - who is amply endowed with strength of arm in the world; who is the most eminent hero in the lineage of the Guptas; whose great splendour is spread far and wide; by whom, practising (good) behaviour, the conduct of those who perform good actions is not obstructed; who is of spotless soul; (and) who is well disciplined in the understanding of musical keys(?):-

(L. 8.) - By whom,-having, with daily intense application, step by step attained his object by means of good behaviour and strength and politic conduct,-instruction in the art of disposition (of resources) was acquired, (and) was employed as the means of (subduing his) enemies who had put themselves forward in the desire for conquest that was so highly welcome (to them):-

(L. 10.) - By whom, when he prepared himself to restore the fallen fortunes of (his) family, a (whole) night was spent on a couch that was the bare earth; and then, having conquered the Puṣyamitras, who had developed great power and wealth, he placed (his) left foot on a foot-stool which was the king (of that tribe himself):-

(L. 11.) - The resplendent behaviour of whom, possessed of spotless fame,-inherent, [but increased] by . . . and patience and heroism which are emphatically unequalled, (and) which destroy the efficacy of the weapons (of his enemies),-is sung in every region by happy men, even down to the children:-

(L. 12.) - Who, when (his) father had attained the skies, conquered (his) enemies by the strength of (his) arm, and established again the ruined fortunes of (his) lineage; and then, crying "the victory has been achieved," betook himself to (his) mother, whose eyes were full of tears from joy, just as Kṛṣṇa, when he had slain (his) enemies, betook himself to (his mother) Devakī;-

(L. 14.) - Who, with his own armies, established (again) (his) lineage that had been made to totter . . . , (and) with his two arms subjugated the earth, (and) shewed mercy to the conquered peoples in distress, (but) has become neither proud nor arrogant, though his glory is increasing day by day; (and) whom the bards raise to distinction with (their) songs and praises:-

(L. 15.) - By whose two arms the earth was shaken, when he, the creator (of a disturbance like that) of a terrible whirlpool, joined in close conflict with the Hūṇas; . . . among enemies . . . arrows . . .

> *.proclaimed . . . just as if it were the roaring of (the river) Gaṅgā, making itself noticed in (their) ears.*
>
> *(L.17.) - . . . the fame of his father . . . (Saying to himself that) an image of some kind or other [should be made], he, the very celebrated one, made this image of that (famous) (god) Śārṅgin, [to endure as long as the moon and stars may last]. And, having here installed this (god), he, whose commands are well-established, has allotted this village (to the idol), in order to increase the religious merit of (his) father.*
>
> *(L. 19.) - Accordingly, this image of the Divine One, and (this village) which has been here agreed to, -both of these, he, the pious-minded one, has assigned for (the increase of) the religious merit of (his) father."*

In line 10, we learn that family fortunes had fallen and Puṣyamitras had developed great power and wealth. The place of Puṣyamitras in Central India was right in the middle of the Imperial Gupta Empire. In line 12, we are told that Skandagupta recovered the ruined fortunes of his lineage by conquering his enemies by the strength of his arm. In line 14, he says again that his lineage had been made to totter and he had to establish it again. We can only imagine how bad things had become while Kumāragupta was sending his messengers of peace to the outside world and getting edicts on Dhamma written all over his empire. Hūṇas considered his policies as an open invitation to plunder. Luckily, they were defeated by Skandagupta as described in line 15, and India received some relief from foreign invasions for the next two decades. Skandagupta assumed the title of Vikramāditya following the victory over the Hūṇas in 170 BCE and established an era to celebrate this occasion. His era became known as the Śūdraka era possibly because of his mother belonging to the Śūdra class. This also explains why Skandagupta chose not to write the name of his mother in his inscriptions. The example of Skandagupta illustrates that a person of any background can rise to the pinnacles of glory if he is given the opportunity.

There is a story about Vikramāditya in Kathāsaritsāgara that fits Skandagupta as the Vikramāditya of the story, and is presented below [4]:

> *"There is in Avanti a famous city, named Ujjayinī, the dwelling-place of Śiva, built by Viśvakarman in the commencement or the Yuga; which, like a virtuous woman, is invincible by strangers; like a lotus-plant is the resort of the goddess of prosperity; like the heart of the good, is rich in virtue; like the earth, is full of many wonderful sights.*
>
> *There dwelt in that city a world-conquering king, named Mahendrāditya, the slayer of his enemies' armies, like Indra in Amarāvatī. In regard of prowess he was a wielder of many weapons; in regard of beauty he was the flower-weaponed god himself; his hand was ever open in bounty, but was firmly clenched on the hilt of his sword. That king had a wife named Saumyadarśanā, who was to him as Śachī to Indra, as Gaurī to Śiva, as Śrī to Vishṇu. And that king had a great minister named Sumati, and a warder named Vajrāyudha, in whose family the office was hereditary. With these the king remained ruling his realm, propitiating Śiva, and ever bearing various vows in order to obtain a son.*
>
> *In the meanwhile, as Śiva was with Pārvatī on the mighty mountain Kailāśa, the glens of which are visited by troops of gods, which is beautiful with the smile that the Northern quarter smiles joyous at vanquishing all the others, all the gods with Indra at their head, came to visit him, being afflicted by the oppression of the Mlechchhas; and the immortals bowed, and then sat down and praised Śiva; and when he asked them the reason of their coming, they addressed to him this prayer: "O god, those Asuras, who were slain by thee and Vishṇu, have been now again born on the earth in the form of Mlechchhas. They slay Brahmans, they interfere with*

the sacrifices and other ceremonies, and they carry off the daughters of hermits: indeed, what crime do not the villains commit? Now, thou knowest, lord, that the world of gods is ever nourished by the earth, for the oblation offered in the fire by Brahmans nourishes the dwellers in heaven. But, as the Mlechchhas have overrun the earth, the auspicious words are nowhere pronounced over the burnt-offering, and the world of gods is being exhausted by the cutting off of their share of the sacrifice and other supplies. So devise an expedient in this matter; cause some hero to become incarnate on the earth, mighty enough to destroy those Mlechchhas."

When Śiva had been thus entreated by the gods, he said to them, "Depart; you need not be anxious about this matter; be at your ease. Rest assured that I will soon devise an expedient which will meet the difficulty." When Śiva had said this, he dismissed the gods to their abodes.

And when they had gone, the Holy one, with Parvati at his side, summoned a Gaṇa, named Mālyavat, and gave him this order, "My son, descend into the condition of a man, and be born in the city of Ujjayinī as the brave son of king Mahendrāditya. That king is a portion of me, and his wife is sprung from a portion of Ambikā; be born in their family, and do the heaven-dwellers the service they require. Slay all those Mlechchhas that obstruct the fulfilment of the law contained in the three Vedas. And by my favour thou shalt be a king ruling over the seven divisions of the world; moreover the Rākṣhasas, the Yakṣhas and the Vetālas shall own thy supremacy; and after thou hast enjoyed human pleasures, thou shalt again return to me."

When the Gaṇa Mālyavat received this command from Siva, he said: "The command of you two divine beings cannot be disobeyed by me; but what enjoyments are there in the life of a man, which involves separations from relations, friends, and servants very hard to bear, and the pain arising from loss of wealth, old age, disease, and the other ills of humanity?" When the Gaṇa said this to Śiva, the god thus replied: "Go, blameless one! These woes shall not fall to thy lot. By my favour thou shalt be happy throughout the whole of thy sojourn on earth." When Śiva said this to Mālyavat, that virtuous Gaṇa immediately disappeared. And he went and was conceived in Ujjayinī, in the proper season, in the womb of the queen of king Mahendrāditya.

And at that time the god, whose diadem is fashioned of a digit of the moon, said to that king in a dream: "I am pleased with thee, king: so a son shall be born to thee, who by his might shall conquer the earth with all its divisions; and that hero shall reduce under his sway the Yakshas, Rākshasas, Piśāchas and others, even those that move in the air, and dwell in Pātāla - and shall slay the hosts of the Mlechchhas; for this reason he shall be named Vikramāditya; and also Vishamaśīla on account of his stern hostility to his enemies."

When the god had said this, he disappeared; and next morning the king woke up, and joyfully related his dream to his ministers. And they also told the king, one after another, with great delight, that Śiva had made a revelation to each of them in a dream that he was to have a son. And at that moment a handmaid of the harem came and showed the king a fruit, saying: "Śiva gave this to the queen in a dream." Then the king rejoiced, saying, again and again: "Truly, Śiva has given me a son," and his ministers congratulated him.

Then his illustrious queen became pregnant, like the eastern quarter in the morning, when the orb of the sun is about to arise, and she was conspicuous for the black tint of the nipples of her breasts, which appeared like a seal to secure the milk for the king with whom she was pregnant. In her dreams at that time she crossed seven seas, being worshipped by all the Yakshas, Vetālas, and Rākshasas. And when the due time was come, she brought forth a glorious son, who lit up the chamber, as the rising sun does the heaven. And when he was born, the sky became indeed glorious, laughing with the falling rain of flowers, and ringing with the noise of the gods' drums. And on that occasion the city was altogether distracted with festive joy, and appeared as if intoxicated, as if possessed by a demon, as if generally wind-struck. And at that time the king rained wealth there so unceasingly, that, except the Buddhists, no one was without a god. And king Mahendrāditya gave him the name of Vikramāditya, which Śiva had mentioned, and also that of Vishamaśīla.

When some more days had passed, there was born to that king's minister, named Sumati, a son of the name of Mahāmati, and the warder Vajrāyudha had a son born to him, named Bhadrāyudha, and the chaplain Mahīdhara had a son of the name of Śrīdhara. And that prince Vikramāditya grew up with those three ministers' sons, as with spirit, courage, and might. When he was invested with the sacred thread, and put under teachers, they were merely the occasions of his learning the sciences, which revealed themselves to him without effort. And whatever science or accomplishment he was seen to employ, was known by those, who understood it, to be possessed by him to the highest degree of excellence. And when people saw that prince fighting with heavenly weapons, they even began to pay less attention to the stories about the great archer Rāma and other heroes of the kind. And his father brought for him beautiful maidens, given by kings who had submitted after defeat, like so many goddesses of Fortune.

Then his father, king Mahendrāditya, seeing that his son was in the bloom of early manhood, of great valour, and beloved by the subjects, duly anointed him heir to his realm, and being himself old, retired with his wife and ministers to Vārāṇasī, and made the god Śiva his refuge.

And king Vikramāditya, having obtained that kingdom of his father, began in due course to blaze forth, as the sun, when it has occupied the sky. Even haughty kings, when they saw the string fitted into the notch of his bending bow, learnt a lesson from that weapon, and bent likewise on every side. Of godlike dignity, having subdued to his sway even Vetālas, Rākshasas and other demons, he chastised righteously those that followed evil courses. The armies of that Vikramāditya roamed over the earth like the rays of the sun, shedding into every quarter the light of order. Though that king was a mighty hero, he dreaded the other world, though a brave warrior, he was not hard-handed; though not uxorious, he was beloved by his wives. He was the father of all the fatherless, the friend of all the friendless, and the protector of all the unprotected among his subjects."

As the father of Vikramāditya is called Mahendrātitya in this story, it is obvious that the story is based on the exploits of Skandagupta Vikramāditya, whose father was Kumāragupta Mahendrātitya. As the slaying of all the Mlechchhas (barbarians) is the theme of this story, it goes without saying that the Hindus were martial, and that they did not subscribe to unilateral pacifism. For the Hindu kings, their honour and the protection of their way of life was a much higher calling than unilateral pacifism. They rejoiced at the defeat of Mlechchhas. If the barbarians dared to attack, their total defeat was the sacred duty of the Hindu kings. In Hindu scriptures, literature as well as inscriptions, the defeat of the Mlechchhas has always been described with joy and pride. Here is what Captain Wilford said about the originators of Hindu eras in 1809 [5]:

"The chronology of its kings is connected with the period of the Caliyuga; which consists of 432,000 years. This, the Hindus have divided into six unequal portions, or subordinate periods, called Śacas, because they derive their origin from six Śacas, or mighty, and glorious monarchs: three of whom have already made their appearance; and three more are expected. This system of the six Śacas, with their periods, is thus explained in the Jyotirvidābharaṇa, an astronomical treatise. Whatever man kills 550,000,000 Śacas (a mighty tribe of Hereticks), becomes a Śaca; and whoever kills this Śaca only, becomes a Śaca also."

Now the number may be exaggerated, but the point is clear. Hindu rulers did not have the slightest compunction in going to war against invading outsiders. Hindu kings celebrated heroism, courage and valour, as did the citizens of their kingdoms.

It is now time to trace the origins and describe the heroic deeds of the greatest hero of them all, the Emperor Vikramāditya, in whose name the Vikrama era has been constituted.

Notes

1. Basham (1982)
2. Wilford (1809b). Quote on pages 152-153.
3. Fleet (1888): 54-56.
4. Penzer (1928): 2-6.
5. Wilford (1809a). Quote on page 82.

"A man, as a general rule, owes very little to what he is born with. A man is what he makes of himself."

- Alexander Graham Bell

6. EMPEROR OF THE HEARTS

After securing the empire from external and internal challenges, Skandagupta Vikramāditya ruled till 161 BCE at which point Narasiṃhagupta, son of Purugupta, became an adult and Skandagupta retired from active political life after handing over the reigns to Narasiṃhagupta. After his retirement, Skandagupta devoted his time to literary pursuits and wrote the play "Mrichchhakatikam". As we have mentioned earlier, Emperor Skandagupta was known as Śūdraka, and an era named Śūdraka era was instituted to celebrate his victory over the Hūṇas. There was peace for over 20 years during which time the reigns of Imperial Gupta empire passed on from Narasiṃhagupta to Kumāragupta II, and then from Kumāragupta II to Budhagupta.

6.1 Emperor Budhagupta

The Eran Stone Pillar Inscription of Budhagupta dated Gupta era 165 (144 BCE) gives us important information to put together the final days of the Imperial Gupta empire [1]:

> *"Victorious is the lord, the four-armed (god Viṣṇu) - whose couch is the broad waters of the four oceans; who is the cause of the continuance, the production, and the destruction, &c., of the universe; (and) whose ensign is Garuḍa!*
>
> *(Line 2.) - In a century of years, increased by sixty-five; and while Budhagupta (is) king; on the twelfth lunar day of the bright*

fortnight of the month Āshāḍha; on the day of Suraguru; (or in figures) the year 100 (and) 60 (and) 5:-

(L. 3.) - And while Suraśmichandra is governing, with the qualities of a regent of one of the quarters of the world, (the country that lies) between the (rivers) Kālindi and Narmadā, (and) is enjoying in the world the glory of (being) a Mahārāja;-

(L. 4.) - On this (lunar day), (specified) as above by the year and month and day; — by the Mahārāja Mātriviṣṇu, who is excessively devoted to the Divine One; who, by the will of (the god) Vidhātṛ, was approached (in marriage-choice) by the goddess of sovereignty, as if by a maiden choosing (him) of her own accord (to be her husband); whose fame extends up to the borders of the four oceans; who is possessed of unimpaired honour and wealth; (and) who has been victorious in battle against many enemies;—who is the son of the son's son of Indraviṣṇu, who was attentive to his duties; who celebrated sacrifices; who practised private study (of the scriptures); who was a Brāhmaṇ saint; (and) who was the most excellent (of the followers) of the Maitrāyaṇīya (sākhā); - who is the son's son of Varuṇaviṣṇu, who imitated the virtuous qualities of (his) father; - (and) who is the son of Hariviṣṇu, who was the counterpart of (his) father in meritorious qualities, (and) was the cause of the advancement of his race;-

(L. 8.) - (By him) and by his younger brother Dhanyaviṣṇu, who is obedient to him, (and) has been accepted with favour by him, - this flag-staff of the divine (god) Janārdana, the troubler of the demons, has been erected, for the purpose of increasing the religious merit of (their) parents.

(L. 9.) - Let prosperity attend all the subjects, headed by the cows and the Brāhmaṇs!"

According to Śrīrāma Goyala, Budhagupta continued to rule till the Gupta era 176 or 495 CE [2]. According to the revised Imperial Gupta era of 309 BCE elaborated in the second chapter of this book, Budhagupta continued to rule till 133 BCE. During the time Budhagupta was ruling, the Śaka ruler Toramāṇa was building his forces to attack India.

6.2 Toramāṇa

Toramāṇa is considered a Hūṇa, though there is no evidence for it. That Toramāṇa was a Śaka, not a Hūṇa, is proven by the name of his son Mihirakula. Mihira is an ancient Persian word which also forms a part of the name of the famous astronomer Varāhamihira, a Śaka Brāhmaṇa, whose ancestors came from Persia. Though there are many literary and inscriptional references to Hūṇas in India, there is hardly any name of the leader of the Hūṇas. This point is significant not only from the point of the history of the Hūṇas, but also for the identification of emperor Vikramāditya of the Vikrama era, whose principal foreign enemy was a Śaka and not a Hūṇa. In the Eran stone boar inscription of Toramāṇa shown below there is no mention of him being a Hūṇa [3]:

> *"Om. Victorious is the god (Viṣṇu), who has the form of a Boar, - who, in the act of lifting up the earth (out of the waters), caused the mountains to tremble with the blows of (his) hard snout; (and) who is the pillar (for the support) of the great house which is three worlds.*
>
> *(Line 1.) – In the first year; while the Mahārājādhirāja, the glorious Toramāṇa, of great fame (and) of great lustre, is governing the earth; -*
>
> *(L. 2.) – On the tenth day of (the month) Phālguna; on this (lunar day), (specified) as above by the regnal year and month and day, (and) invested as above with its own characteristics; -*
>
> *(L. 3.) – By Dhanyaviṣṇu, - the younger brother, obedient to him (and) accepted with favour by him, of the Mahārāja Mātṛviṣṇu, who has gone to heaven, who was excessively devoted to the Divine One; who, by the will of (the god) Vidhātṛ, was approached (in*

> *marriage-choice) by the goddess of sovereignty, as if by a maiden choosing (him) of her own accord (to be her husband); whose fame extended up to the borders of the four oceans; who was possessed of unimpaired honour and wealth; (and) who was victorious in battle against many enemies; who was the son of the son's son of Indraviṣṇu, who was attentive to his duties, who celebrated sacrifices; who practiced private study (of the scriptures); who was a Brāhmaṇ saint; (and) who was the most excellent (of the followers of) of the Maitrāyaṇiya (sākhā); who was the son's son of Varuṇaviṣṇu, who imitated the virtuous qualities of (his) father in meritorious qualities, (and) was the cause of the advancement of his race;*
>
> *(L. 6.) – (By this Dhanyaviṣṇu) accomplishing, in unison with (the previously expressed wishes of) him, a joint deed of religious merit, for the sake of increasing the religious merit of (his) parents, this stone temple of the divine (god) Nārāyaṇa, who has the form of a boar (and) who is entirely devoted to (the welfare of) the universe, has been caused to be made in this his own viṣaya of Airikiṇa.*
>
> *(L. 8.) – Let prosperity attend all the subjects, headed by the cows and the Brāhmaṇs.*

This inscription was written during the first year of the rule of Toramāṇa and is from the same area where the inscription of Budhagupta was found. This inscription proves that Toramāṇa made extensive inroads inside the Imperial Gupta Empire. Eran is located in the Sagar district in Madhya Pradesh, almost in the centre of India. The inscription tells us that Toramāṇa had appointed Dhanyaviṣṇu, the younger brother of Mahārāja Mātṛviṣṇu, to rule Eran. Mahārāja Mātṛviṣṇu, who was ruling Eran under the lordship of Budhagupta, had gone to heaven. It can be concluded then that during the final days of the rule of Budhagupta, a battle was fought in Eran between the forces of Budhagupta and Toramāṇa in which Toramāṇa emerged victorious. Mahārāja Mātṛviṣṇu died fighting and Toramāṇa appointed his younger brother Dhanyaviṣṇu to rule this area. As the war was fought during the final days of the rule of Budhagupta, it took place circa 133 BCE. This date is also corroborated from an inscription of Emperor Prakāśadharmā. As the sun was setting on the Imperial Gupta Empire, a new dynasty was emerging out of its shadows to protect India from foreign invaders, and in this dynasty was born the Emperor of Indian hearts, Emperor Vikramāditya.

6.3 Rise of the Aulikaras

About 350 km west of Eran and 150 km northwest of Ujjain is the city of Mandsaur in the Malwa region in the state of Madhya Pradesh. The ancient name of this city was Daśapura. The history of Aulikaras starts here with Jayavardhana, who has been called Narendra. The name Narendra is a combination of the words Nara meaning man and Indra, King of Gods. Thus Narendra means kingly man, but we cannot be sure whether Jayavardhana was a king or his descendants have used this title to just show respect for him. Siṃhavarman was next in line and he was a king under the Lordship of the Imperial Guptas. We don't know the exact dates of the rule of Jayavardhana and Siṃhavarman, but judging from the date of Naravarman (Mālava 461 and 474), the Aulikara family started the long journey to become the paramount power of India during the reign of Samudragupta.

Table 6.1 shows the proposed timeline of Aulikara family along with the currently accepted dates. The data for Table 6.1 is taken from the genealogical chart prepared by Richard Soloman in the article, "New Inscriptional Evidence for the History of the Aulikaras of Mandasor" [4]. There were different families of Aulikaras, who gained prominence in succession. The rule of the first Aulikara family ended with Prabhākara, whose date is Mālava 524 or 178 BCE. This brings us to the second Aulikara family, in which Emperor Vikramāditya was born.

Table 6.1: The proposed timeline of the Aulikara family

Name	Date	Accepted Chronology [4]	Proposed chronology	Comments
Naravarman	Mālava 461, 474	404 CE, 417 CE	241 BCE, 228 BCE	Aulikara line 1
Viśvavarman	Kṛta 480	423 CE	222 BCE	Aulikara line 1
Bandhuvarman	Mālava 493	436 CE	209 BCE	Aulikara line 1
Prabhākara	Mālava 524	467 CE	178 BCE	Aulikara line 1
Prakāśadharmā	Mālava 572	515 CE	130 BCE	Aulikara line 2
Yaśodharmā	Mālava 589	532 CE	113 BCE	Aulikara line 2

The genealogy of this Aulikara family is given in the Rīsthal Inscription of Emperor Prakāśadharmā [4]. The first person mentioned in this Aulikara line was General Dramavardhana, who has also been called Narendra. His son was king Jayavardhana. His son was king Ajitavardhana, whose son was Vibhīṣaṇavardhana. His son was Rājyavardhana, whose son was Prakāśadharmā, a crest of kings. Prakāśadharmā defeated Toramāṇa, Lord of the Hūṇas, in battle. Prakāśadharmā constructed the Vibhīṣaṇa Lake and dedicated to his grandfather Vibhīṣaṇavardhana. At the command of Prakāśadharmā, his viceroy Bhagvaddoṣa constructed the Prakāśeśvara temple, a symbol of Bhāratavarṣa (India). The inscription was made in the year 572. The eulogy was composed by Vasula, son of Kakka.

For a complete transcript of the inscription, the reader is referred to the article "New Inscriptional Evidence for the History of the

Aulikaras of Mandasor" by Richard Soloman [4]. As the inscription was made in the Mālava year 572, Toramāṇa was defeated by Prakāśadharmā before the year 130 BCE. Toramāṇa was succeeded by his son Mihirakula.

6.4 Mihirakula

By all accounts, Mihirakula was a cruel emperor. Buddhist traveler Xuan Zang (Hiuen Tsiang) has accused him of persecution of the Buddhists and destruction of the monasteries. Kalhaṇa says in Rājataraṅgiṇī that Mihirakula had killed 30 million people [5]. That Mihirakula had made deep inroads inside India is evident from the following Stone Inscription of Mihirakula from Gwalior in Madhya Pradesh [6]:

> *"[Om!] May he (the Sun) protect you, who is victorious, dispelling the darkness of the banks of clouds with the masses of the multitude of his rays that light up the sky; (and) decorating the top of the side of the mountain of dawn with (his) horses, which have the tossing ends of (their) manes disheveled through the fatigue (induced) by (their) startled gait;-(and) who,-having (his) chariot-wheels (?) swallowed (?) ... the mountain of dawn; dispelling distress; (being) the light of the house which is the world; (and) effecting the destruction of night,-creates the fresh beauty of the water-lilies by (his) rays which are of the colour of molten gold.*
>
> *(Line 2.) – (There was) a ruler of [the earth], of great merit, who was renowned by the name of the glorious Toramāṇa; by whom, through (his) heroism that was specially characterized by truthfulness, the earth was governed with justice.*
>
> *(L. 3.) – Of him, the fame of whose family has risen high, the son (is) he, of unequalled prowess, the lord of the earth, who is renowned under the name of Mihirakula, (and) who, (himself) unbroken, [broke the power of] Paśupati.*

(L. 4.) – While [he], the king, the remover of distress, possessed of large and pellucid eyes, is governing the earth; in the augmenting reign, (and) in the fifteenth year, of (him) the best of kings; the month Kārttika, cool and fragrant with the perfume of the red and blue waterlilies that are caused to blossom by the smiles of the rays of the moon, having come; while the spotless moon is shining; and a very auspicious day, - heralded by the chiefs of the classes of the twice-born with the noise of the proclamation of a holy day, (and) possessed of the (proper) tithi and nakṣhatra and muhūrta,- having arrived;-

(L. 5.) – The son's son of Matritula, and the son of Mātridāsa, by the name Mātricheṭa, an inhabitant of ... on the hill, has caused to be made, on the delightful mountain which is speckled with various metals and has the appellation of Gopa, a stone-temple, the chief among the best of temples, of the Sun, for the purpose of increasing the religious merit of (his) parents and of himself, and of those who, by the ... of the king, dwell on this best of mountains.

(L. 7.) – Those who cause to be made an excellent house of the Sun, like in lustre to the rays of the moon, their abode is in heaven, until the destruction of all things!

(L. 7.) – (This) very famous proclamation of the true religion has been composed through devotion to the Sun, by him who is renowned by the name of Keśava and by ... ditya.

(L. 8.) – As long as the moon shines on the thicket that is the knot of the braided hair of (the god) Śarva; and as long as the mountain Meru continues to have (its) slopes adorned by the feet of the nymphs of heaven; and as long as (the god) Viṣṇu bears the radiant (goddess) Śrī upon (his) breast which is like a dark-blue cloud;so long (this) chief of [stone]-temples shall stand upon the delightful summit of the hill!"

This inscription was written in the 15th year of the rule of Mihirakula. We have seen that his father Toramāṇa was defeated by Prakāśadharmā shortly before 130 BCE. If Mihirakula took over the reign shortly after the defeat of Toramāṇa in 130 BCE, then this inscription was written shortly before 115 BCE. Sometime after this date Mihirakula was defeated by Emperor Yaśodharmā. It is the defeat of the Śaka king Mihirakula by Yaśodharmā that gave him the title Śakāri (Enemy of the Śakas) Vikramāditya.

6.5 Yaśodharmā the Great

There are two inscriptions that give us information about Emperor Yaśodharmā Viṣṇuvardhana. The Mandasor stone inscription of Yaśodharmā was recovered from a well in Mandsaur and is as follows [7]:

> *"Perfection has been attained! Victorious is he, (the god) Pinākin, the lord of (all) the worlds, - in whose songs, hummed with smiles, the splendor of (his) teeth, like the luster of lightning sparkling in the night, envelops and brings into full view all this universe! May he, (the god) Śambhū, confer many auspicious gifts upon you, - employed by whom in the rites of (effecting the) continuance and the destruction and the production of (all) things that exist, (the god) Svayambhū, is obedient to (his) commands, for the sake of the maintenance of (all) the worlds; and by whom, leading (him) to dignity in the world, he has been brought to the condition of being the father (of the universe)! May the serpent of the creator of existence accomplish the allayment of your distress, - (that serpent) the multitude of whose foreheads, bowed down afar by the pressure of the heavy weight of the jewels in (their) hoods, obscures the radiance of the moon (on his master's forehead); (and) who (with the folds of his body) binds securely on (his master's) head the chaplet of bones which is full of holes (for stringing them). May the creator of waters, which was dug out by the sixty thousands sons of Sagara, (and) which possesses a lustre equal to (that of) the sky, preserve for a long time the glories of this best of wells.*

(Line 4.) – Now, victorious is that tribal ruler, having the name of the glorious Yasodharmā, who having plunged into the army of (his) enemies, as if into a grove of thornapple-trees, (and) having bent down the reputations of heroes like the tender creepers of trees, effects the adornment of (his) body with the fragments of young sprouts which are the wounds (inflicted on him).

(L 5.) – And, again, victorious over the earth is this same king of men, the glorious Vishṇuvardhana, the conqueror in war; by whom his own famous lineage, which has the aulikara-crest, has been brought to a state of dignity that is ever higher and higher. By him, having brought into subjection, with peaceful overtures and by war, the very mighty kings of the east and many (kings) of the north, this second name of "supreme king of kings and supreme lord" pleasing in the world (but) difficult of attainment, is carried on high. Through him, having conquered the earth with (his own) arm, many countries, in which the sun is obscured by the smoke, resembling dense dark blue clouds, of the oblations of the sacrifices; (and) which abound with thick and thriving crops through (the god) Maghavan pouring cloudfuls of rain upon (their) boundaries; (and) in which the ends of the fresh sprouts of the mango trees in the parks are eagerly plucked in joy by the hands of wanton women, - enjoy the happiness of being possessed of a good king. Though the dust, grey like the hide of an ass, stirred up by his armies, which have (their) banners lifted on high; (and) which have the lodhra trees tossed about in all directions by the tusks of (their) infuriated elephants; (and) which have the crevices of the Vindhya mountains made resonant with the noise of (their) journeying through the forests, - the orb of the sun appears dark (and) dull-rayed, as if it were an eye in a peacock's tail reversed.

(L. 9.) - The servant of the kings who founded the family of that lord, was Shashṭhidatta, -the fame of whose religious merit was known far and wide through the protection of (their) feet; who by his resoluteness conquered the six enemies (of religion); (and) who was indeed very excellent. As the torrent, flowing high and low, of

(the river) Gaṅgā (spreads abroad) from (the mountain) Himavat, (and) the extensive mass of the waters of (the river) Revā from the moon, - (so) from him, whose dignity was manifested, there spreads a pure race of Naigamas, most worthy to be sought in fellowship.

(L. 11.) – of him, from a wife of good family, there was born a son, resembling him (in good qualities), the source of fame, - whom, (being named) Varāhadāsa, (and) being full of self control (and) of great worth, people speak of as if he were an (incarnate) portion of (the god) Hari.

(L. 11.) – As it it were the sun (illuminating) the mightly summit of a mountain, Ravikirtti with the wealth of his character illumined that family, which was made eminent by men who combined good actions with worldly occupations; which had its foundations well established in the earth; (and) which maintained a very firm position of endurance that was free from (any risk of) being broken; (Ravikīrtti), by whom, sustaining the pure (and) undeviating path of traditional law that is acceptable to good people, nobility of birth was not made a thing of false assertion (even) in the Kali age. From him, (his) chaste wife Bhānuguptā gave birth to three sons, who dispelled the darkness (of ignorance) with the rays of (their) intellects, as if (she had produced three) sacrifices from a fire.

(L. 13.) – The first was Bhagavaddoṣa, the prop of his relatives in the paths of religious actions, just as Uddhava (was) of the Andhakas, - who was a very Vedhas in displaying much prudence in the hard-to-be-traversed path of the meaning (of words); who, like Vidura, always looked far ahead with deliberation; (and) who is with great pleasure sung of by poets, in Sanskrit and Prakrit construction of the arrangements of sentences as being well versed in speech.

(L. 15.) – And after him there came that (well known) Abhayadatta, maintaining a high position on the earth, (and) collecting (in order to dispel it) the fear of (his) subjects (?); - by whose eyes of intellect, which served him like the eyes of a spy, no

trifle however remote, remained undetected, (even) at night; (Abhayadatta), of fruitful actions, who like (Brihaspati) the preceptor of the gods, to the advantage of those who belonged to the (four recognized) castes, with the functions of a Rājasthaniya protected the region, containing many countries presided over by his own upright counselors, which lies between the Vindhya (mountains), from the slopes of the summits of which there flows the pale mass of the waters of (the river) Revā, and the mountain Pāriyātra, on which the trees are bent down in (their) frolicsome leaps by the long-tailed monkeys, (and stretches) up to the western ocean.

(L. 17.) – Now he, Dharmadoṣa, the son of Doṣakumbha, - by whom this kingdom has been made, as if (it were still) in the Kṛta age, free from any intermixture of all the castes, (and peaceable through) having hostilities allayed, (and) undisturbed by care, - in accordance with justice proudly supports the burden (of government) that had (previously) been borne by him; (Dharmadoṣa), who, - not being too eager about his own comfort, (and) bearing, for the sake of his lord, in the difficult path (of administration), the burden (of government), very heavily weighted and not shared by another, - wears royal apparel only as mark of distinction (and not for his own pleasure), just as a bull carries a wrinkled pendulous dew-lap.

(L. 19.) – His younger brother, Dakṣha, - invested with the decoration of the protection of friends, as if he were (his) broad shouldered (right) arm (decorated) with choice jewels; (and) bearing the name of "the faultless one," which causes great joy to the ear and heart, caused to be excavated this great well. This great (and) skillful work was achieved here by him, who is of great intellect, for the sake of his paternal uncle, the beloved Abhayadatta, who was cut off (before his time) by the mighty god Kṛtānta, just as if he were a tree, the shade of which is pleasant to resort to (and) which yields fruits that are salutary and sweet through ripeness, (wantonly) destroyed by a lordly elephant.

(L. 21.) – Five hundred autumns, together with ninety less by one, having elapsed from (the establishment of) the supremacy of the tribal constitution of the Mālavas, (and) being written down in order to determine the (present) time; in the season in which the songs, resembling the arrows of (the god) Smara, of the cuckoos, whose utterances are low and tender, cleave open, as it were, the minds of those who are far away from home; and in which the humming of the flights of bees, sounding low on account of the burden (that they carry), is heard through the woods, like the resounding bow of (the god Kāmadeva) who has the banner of flowers, when its string is caused to vibrate; - in the season in which there is the month of the coming on of flowers, when the wind, soothing the affectionate (but) perverted thoughts of disdainful women who are angry with their lovers, as if they were charming fresh sprouts arrayed in colours, devotes itself to breaking down (their) pride, in that season this (well) was caused to be constructed.

(L. 24.) – As long as the ocean, embracing with (its) lofty waves, as if with long arms, the orb of the moon, which has its full assemblage of rays (and is more) lovely (than ever) from contact (with the waters), maintains friendship (with it), so long let this excellent well endure, possessing a surrounding enclosure of lines at the edge of the masonry work, as if it were a garland worn around a shaven head, (and) discharging pure waters the flavor of which is equal to nectar.

(L. 25.) – May this intelligent Daksha for a long time protect this act of piety, (he who is) skillful, true to (his) promises, modest, brave, attentive to old people, grateful, full of energy, unwearied in the business matters of (his) lord (and) faultless. (This eulogy) has been engraved by Govinda."

This inscription was written in Mālava year 589, which is 113 BCE, according to the Mālava/Kṛta era starting in 702 BCE as discussed in Chapter 2 of this book. It tells us that the full name of the emperor was Yaśodharmā Viṣṇuvardhana and he belonged to the Aulikara clan. He had brought into subjection, with peaceful overtures and by war, the very mighty kings of the east and many (kings) of the north. With these victories he had justifiably taken the title of "supreme king of kings and supreme lord". His army had crossed the Vindhya Mountain and hence he had won territories in South India as well by 113 BCE. The important question is whether he had defeated Mihirakula by this time. We have seen above that Gwalior in Madhya Pradesh was under the control of Mihirakula. This is proven beyond doubt by inscriptional as well as numismatic evidence. Gwalior is little over 500 km north east of Mandsaur. As this inscription claims that by 113 BCE Yaśodharmā had conquered the mighty kings of the east and many kings of the north, it is most likely that he had already defeated Mihirakula by this time.

The second inscription of Yaśodharmā gives evidence of his victory over Mihirakula but is not dated. The full transcript of this important inscription called "Mandasor Pillar Inscription of Yaśodharmā" is as follows [8]:

"May that very long banner of (the god) Śūlapāṇi destroy the glory of your enemies; - (that banner) which bears (a representation of) the bull (Nandi), marked by the five fingers (dipped in some dye and then) placed on him by (Pārvatī) the daughter of the mountain (Himālaya), who causes the distant regions, in which the demons are driven wild with fear by (his) terrible bellowings, to shake; (and) who makes the glens of (the mountain) Sumeru to have their rocks split open by the blows of his horns!

(Line 2.) - He, to whose arm, as if (to the arm) of (the god) Shārngapāṇi, the fore-arm of which is marked with callous parts caused by the hard string of (his) bow, (and) which is steadfast in the successful carrying out of vows for the benefit of mankind, the earth betook itself (for succour), when it was afflicted by kings of the present age, who manifested pride; who were cruel through

want of proper training; who, from delusion, transgressed the path of good conduct; (and) who were destitute of virtuous delights:

(L. 3.) - He who, in this age which is the ravisher of good behaviour, through the action simply of (his good) intentions shone gloriously, not associating with other kings who adopted a reprehensible course of conduct, just as an offering of flowers (is beautiful when it is not laid down) in the dust; he in whom, possessed of a wealth of virtue, (and so) falling but little short of Manu and Bharata and Alarka and Māndhātri, the title of "universal sovereign" shines more (than in any other), like a resplendent jewel (set) in good gold.

(L. 4.) - He who, spurning (the confinement of) the boundaries of his own house, enjoys those countries, thickly covered over with deserts and mountains and trees and thickets and rivers and strong-armed heroes, (and) having (their) kings assaulted by (his) prowess, - which were not enjoyed (even) by the lords of the Guptas, whose prowess was displayed by invading the whole (remainder of the) earth, (and) which the command of the chiefs of the Hūṇas , that established itself on the tiaras of (many) kings, failed to penetrate.

(L. 5.) - He before whose feet chieftains, having (their) arrogance removed by the strength of (his) arm, bow down, from the neighbourhood of the (river) Lauhitya up to (the mountain) Mahendra, the lands at the foot of which are impenetrable through the groves of palmyra-trees, (and) from (Himālaya) the mountain of snow, the tablelands of which are embraced by the (river) Gangā, up to the Western Ocean, by which (all) the divisions of the earth are made of various hues through the intermingling of the rays of the jewels in the locks of hair on the tops of (their) heads.

(L.6.) - He by whom (his) head has never been brought into the humility of obeisance to any other save (the god) Sthāṇu; he, through the embraces of whose arms (Himālaya) the mountain of snow carries no longer the pride of the title of being a place that is difficult of access; he to whose two feet respect was paid, with complimentary presents of the flowers from the lock of hair on the

top of (his) head, by even that (famous) king Mihirakula, whose forehead was pained through being bent low down by the strength of (his) arm in (the act of compelling) obeisance.

(L. 7.) - By him, the king, the glorious Yashodharmā, the firm beams of whose arms are as charming as pillars, this column, which shall endure to the time of the destruction of the world, has been erected here, as if to measure out the earth; as if to enumerate on high the multitude of the heavenly lights; (and) as if to point out the path of his own fame to the skies above, acquired by good actions; (this column) which shines refulgent, as if it were a lofty arm of the earth, raised up in joy to write upon the surface of the moon the excellence of the virtues of Yashodharmā, to the effect that – "His birth (is) in a lineage that is worthy to be eulogised; there is seen in him a charming behaviour that is destructive of sin; he is the abode of religion; (and) the (good) customs of mankind continue current, unimpeded (in any way) by him."

(L. 9.) - From a desire thus to praise this king, of meritorious actions, (these) verses have been composed by Vāsula, the son of Kakka. (This eulogy) has been engraved by Govinda."

This inscription gives more details of the exploits of Emperor Yaśodharmā Viṣṇuvardhana. He ruled over territories that were not part of the mighty Gupta Empire. He had subdued the chiefs of the Hūṇas. He had conquered the territories up to the river Lauhitya and the mountain Mahendra. Lauhitya is another name for the Brahmaputra River, which starts from Tibet and flows through Arunachal Pradesh, Assam and Bangladesh. There are two mountains that can be identified with Mahendra, one in Orissa and another in Tamil Nadu. Since the eastern boundary of Yaśodharmā's empire is already given as the Brahmaputra River, there is no need for another landmark in the east. The Mahendra then needs to be identified with the mountain of the same name in the Tirunelveli district in Tamil Nadu. This is close to the southern tip of India. He further states that his empire extended up to the Himālaya and in the west up to the ocean.

We can see that this inscription gives the boundaries of his empire in all four directions. This is again confirmed by referring to all the divisions of the earth. We now get the feel for the pan-Indian empire of Yaśodharmā Viṣṇuvardhana and realize that he was not exaggerating when he claimed that he ruled over the territories not even enjoyed by the Imperial Guptas. Here is an emperor who not only united all of India under one rule, but went beyond India's borders all the way to Bactria, as we will see shortly. No wonder people celebrated his achievements and made him the hero of the most endearing legends of ancient India.

The crowning glory of his achievement was the defeat of Mihirakula, who was a Śaka, as his name suggests. History books tell us that Mihirakula and his father Toramāṇa were Hūṇas. The claim is based on the evidence of this inscription under discussion. But there is nothing in this inscription that tells us that Mihirakula was a Hūṇa. Hūṇas are referred to in Line 4, while Mihirakula is referred to in Line 6, and in between there is Line 5 that describes the boundaries of Yaśodharmā's empire in the four directions. There is nothing in Line 5 that connects Line 4 and Line 6. The inscription clearly makes no connection between the chief of the Hūṇas and Mihirakula. Even if Mihirakula is referred as the king of the Hūṇas, it does not make Mihirakula a Hūṇa automatically. The king of the Hūṇas must not necessarily be a Hūṇa himself, just like king of the Indians during British rule was not an Indian. The following comments are truly revealing in this regard [9]:

> *"In the Mandasor inscription of Yaśodharman reference is made both to Mihirakula and to the Hūṇas, but in a manner which far from connecting the two, might even suggest a definite distinction between them.... This belief rests solely upon the identification of Toramāṇa and Mihirakula (also called Mihiragula) as Hūṇa leaders. Although this view is generally assumed, there is no definitive*

> *evidence in support of it, and we cannot altogether rule out the possibility that Toramāṇa was a Kuṣāṇa chief, and being allied to the Hūṇas, was mistaken as such in India, specially because he led the Hūṇa hordes."*

There is a detailed story about Mihirakula in the writing of Xuan Zang (Hiuen Tsiang). Let us try to see how this story fits in the light of the evidence presented so far. The details given by Hiuen Tsiang are as follows [10]:

> *"To the south-west of the capital about 14 or 15 li we come to the old town of Śākala (She-kie-lo). Although its walls are thrown down, the foundations are still firm and strong. It is about 20 li in circuit. In the midst of it they have built a little town of about 6 or 7 li in circuit; the inhabitants are prosperous and rich. This was the old capital of the country. Some centuries ago there was a king called Mo-hi-lo-kiu-lo (Mahirakula), who established his authority in this town and ruled over India. He was of quick talent, and naturally brave. He subdued all the neighboring provinces without exception. In his intervals of leisure he desired to examine the law of Buddha, and he commanded that one among the priests of superior talent should wait on him. Now it happened that none of the priests dared to attend to his command. Those who had few desires and were content, did not care about distinction; those of superior learning and high renown despised the royal bounty (glitter). At this time there was an old servant in the king's household who had long worn the religious garments. He was of distinguished ability and able to enter on discussion, and was very eloquent. The priests put him forward in answer to the royal appeal. The king said, "I have respect for the law of Buddha, and I invited from far any renowned priest (to come and instruct me), and now the congregation have put forward this servant to discuss with me. I always thought that amongst the priests there were men of illustrious ability; after what has happened to-day what further respect can I have for priesthood?" He then issued an edict to*

destroy all the priests through the five Indies, to overthrow the law of Buddha, and leave nothing remaining.

Bālāditya-rāja, king of Magadha, profoundly honoured the law of Buddha and tenderly nourished his people. When he heard of the cruel persecution and atrocities of Mahirakula (Ta-tso), he strictly guarded the frontiers of his kingdom and refused to pay tribute. Then Mahirakula raised an army to punish his rebellion. Bālāditya-rāja, knowing his renown, said to his ministers, "I hear that these thieves are coming, and I cannot fight with them (their troops); by the permission of my ministers I will conceal my poor person among the bushes of the morass." Having said this, he departed from his palace and wandered through the mountains and deserts. Being very much beloved in his kingdom, his followers amounted to many myriads, who fled with him and hid themselves in the islands of the sea.

Mahirakula-rāja, committing his army to his younger brother, himself embarked on the sea to go attack Bālāditya. The king guarding the narrow passes, whilst the light cavalry were out to provoke the enemy to fight, sounded the golden drum, and his soldiers suddenly rose on every side and took Mahirakula alive as captive, and brought him into the presence (of Bālāditya).

The king Mahirakula being overcome with shame at his defeat, covered his face with his robe. Bālāditya sitting on his throne with his ministers round him, ordered one of them to tell the king to uncover himself as he wished to speak with him.

Mahirakula answered, "The subject and the master have changed places; that enemies should look on one another is useless; and what advantage is there in seeing my face during conversation?"

Having given the order three times with no success, the king the ordered his crimes to be published, and said, "The field of religious merit connected with the three precious objects of reverence is a public blessing; but this you have overturned and destroyed like a wild beast. Your religious merit is over, and unprotected by fortune you are my prisoner. Your crimes admit no extenuation and you must die."

At this time the mother of Bālāditya was of wide celebrity on account of her vigorous intellect and her skill in casting horoscopes. Hearing that they were going to kill Mahirakula, she addressed Bālāditya -rāja and said, "I have understood that Mahirakula is of remarkable beauty and vast wisdom. I should like to see him once."

Bālāditya -rāja (Yeou-jih) ordered them to bring in Mahirakula to the presence of his mother in her palace. Then she said, "Alas! Mahirakula, be not ashamed! Worldly things are impermanent; success and discomfiture follow one another according to circumstances. I regard myself as your mother and you as my son; remove the covering from your face and speak to me."

Mahirakula said, "A little while ago I was prince of a victorious country, now I am a prisoner condemned to death. I have lost my kingly estate and I am unable to offer my religious services; I am ashamed in the presence of my ancestors and of my people. In very truth I am ashamed before all, whether before heaven or earth. I find no deliverance. Therefore I hide my face with my mantle." The mother of the king said, "Prosperity or the opposite depends on the occasion; gain and loss come in turn. If you give way to events (things), you are lost; but if you rise above circumstances, though you fall, you may rise again. Believe me, the result of deeds depends on the occasion. Lift the covering from your face and speak with me. I may perhaps save your life."

Mahirakula, thanking her, said, "I have inherited a kingdom without having the necessary talent for government, and so I have abused the royal power in inflicting punishment; for this reason I have lost my kingdom. But though I am in chains, yet I desire life if only for a day. Let me thank you with uncovered face for your offer of safety." Whereupon he removed his mantle and showed his face. The king's mother said, "My son is well-favoured; he will die after his years are accomplished." Then she said to Bālāditya, "In agreement with former regulation, it is right to forgive crime and to love to give life. Although Mihirakula has long accumulated sinful actions, yet his remnant of merit is not altogether exhausted. If you kill this man, for twelve years you will see him with his pale face before you. I gather from his air that he will be the king of a small country; let him rule over some small kingdom in the north."

Then Bālāditya -rāja, obeying his dear mother's command, had pity on the prince bereft of his kingdom; gave him in marriage to a young maiden and treated him with extreme courtesy. Then he assembled the troops he has left and added a guard to escort him from the island.

Mihirakula-rāja's brother having gone back, established himself in the kingdom. Mahirakula having lost his royal estate, concealed himself in the isles and deserts, and going northwards to Kaśmīr, he sought there an asylum. The king of Kaśmīr received him with honour, and moved with pity for his loss, gave him a small territory and a town to govern. After some years he stirred up the people of the town to rebellion, and killed the king of Kaśmīr and placed himself on the throne. Profiting by this victory and the renown it got him, he went to the west, plotting against the kingdom of Gandhāra. He set some soldiers in ambush and took and killed the king. He exterminated the royal family and the chief minister, overthrew the stūpas, destroyed the saṅghārāmas, altogether one thousand six hundred foundations. Besides those whom his soldiers had killed there were nine hundred thousand whom he was about to destroy without leaving one. At this time all the ministers addressed him and said, "Great king! your prowess has gained a great victory, and our soldiers are no longer engaged in conflict. Now that you have punished the chief, why would you charge the poor people with fault? Let us, insignificant as we are die, in their stead."

The king said, "You believe in the law of Buddha and greatly reverence the mysterious law of merit. Your aim is to arrive at the condition of Buddha, and then you will declare fully, under the form of Jatakas, my evil deeds for the good of future generations. Now go back to your estates, and say no more on the subject."

Then he slew three ten myriads of people of the first rank by the side of the Sin-tu river; the same number of the middle rank he drowned in the river, and the same number of the third rank he divided among his soldiers (as slaves). Then he took the wealth of the country he had destroyed, assembled his troops, and returned. But before the year was out he died. At the time of his death there was thunder and hail and a thick darkness; the earth shook and a mighty tempest raged. Then the holy saints said in pity, "For having killed countless victims and overthrown the law of Buddha, he has now fallen into the lowest hell, where he shall pass endless ages of revolution."

Even in the framework of accepted chronology, historians have had a tough time reconciling the statement of Hiuen Tsiang with inscriptional evidence cited in this chapter. First of all, Hiuen Tsiang says that the time of Mihirakula was some centuries before his arrival in India, but he came to India just after a century from Mihirakula's time, according to modern history. Clearly, his testimony favours the chronology developed in this book. Second, the example of Bālāditya shows that the Buddhist rulers were cowards in general and their first instinct was to run away and hide when attacked by invaders instead of facing them and protecting the people, which is supposed to be the foremost duty of a king.

Since Hiuen Tsiang came several centuries after the event, was a foreigner with not a very good understanding of Indian history, and on top of that was trying to justify Buddhist beliefs in real life events, all that can be said is that he was totally confused, and it is difficult to make sense out of this story. Bālāditya could not have defeated Mihirakula as per the inscription of Yaśodharmā, Mihirakula had never bowed his head before anyone up to his defeat by Yaśodharmā. Yaśodharmā could not be subordinate to Bālāditya, as his father Prakāśadharmā already was an independent king with the title of Adhirāja. One possibility is that the first part of the story refers to Toramāṇa, and the second part of the story refers to Mihirakula. It was Toramāṇa who had attacked Bālāditya, and Bālāditya fled. Prakāśadharmā then came forward, defeated Toramāṇa, and declared independence. Later when Mihirakula was captured and paraded by Yaśodharmā, his mother felt pity on Mihirakula and asked Yaśodharmā to free Mihirakula.

We have another piece of evidence that has a bearing on the turn of events under consideration. This evidence is the "Eran Posthumous Stone Pillar Inscription of Goparāja," and is quoted below [11]:

> *"Om! In a century of years, increased by ninety-one; on the seventh lunar day of the dark fortnight of (the month) Srāvana; (or in figures) the year 100 (and) 90 (and) 1; (the month) Srāvana; the dark fortnight; the day 7...*
>
> *(Line 2.) - (There was) a king, renowned under the name of . . . rāja, sprung from the ... laksha (?) lineage; and his son (was) that very valorous king (who was known) by the name (of) Mādhava.*
>
> *(L. 3.) - His son was the illustrious Goparāja, renowned for manliness; the daughter's son of the Sarabha king; who is (even) now (?) the ornament of (his) lineage.*
>
> *(L. 5.) - (There is) the glorious Bhānugupta, the bravest man on the earth, a mighty king, equal to Pārtha, exceedingly heroic; and, along with him, Goparāja followed . . . (his) friends (and came) here. [And] having fought a very famous battle, he, [who was but little short of being equal to] the celestial [king (Indra)], (died and) went to heaven; and (his) devoted, attached, beloved, and beauteous wife, in close companionship, accompanied (him) onto the funeral pyre."*

The ruling monarch on the side of Goparāja is mentioned as Bhānugupta, and the year is mentioned as 191. Since the ruling monarch is a Gupta, it can be assumed that the era under consideration is the Gupta era. According to the Imperial Gupta era starting in 309 BCE, year 191 of this era will fall in 118 BCE. The question is, who was the adversary that Bhānugupta and Goparāja were fighting? Based on the discussion in this chapter, we already know that Toramāṇa was defeated by Prakāśadharmā before 130 BCE, and Mihirakula was defeated by Yaśodharmā before 113 BCE. In between 130 BCE and 113 BCE, Mihirakula ruled for 15 years. It seems that the likely sequence of events is as follows: shortly before 130 BCE Imperial Guptas were attacked by Toramāṇa. The Gupta ruler fled and hid somewhere. While Toramāṇa was returning, he was attacked by Prakāśadharmā, who was a subordinate of the Gupta ruler. Toramāṇa lost the battle and Prakāśadharmā declared independence from the Gupta ruler. After Toramāṇa's defeat at the hands of Prakāśadharmā, Toramāṇa's son Mihirakula took over the empire. Yaśodharmā was probably less than ten-years-old at this time as he died in 57 BCE, some 73 years later. Mihirakula took time to build his military strength and attacked the Imperial Gupta ruler Bhānugupta in 118 BCE. Bhānugupta was defeated and Goparāja lost his life in the battle. It fell on the Aulikaras then to defend India from the cruel Śaka ruler Mihirakula. By this time Yaśodharmā was in his twenties and raring to defend India from the Śakas and other foreign rulers. Prakāśadharmā handed over the reign to his son Yaśodharmā with a directive to make Bhārata (India) free of Mlechchhas, the despised barbarian foreigners. Sometime before 113 BCE, a decisive battle was fought between Yaśodharmā and Mihirakula in which Mihirakula's forces were totally uprooted. Mihirakula had to put his head on Yaśodharmā's feet and beg for mercy. Yaśodharmā spared his life respecting his mother's wish, but took direct control over his kingdom.

After making sure that Mihirakula posed no danger to him, Yaśodharmā embarked on a mission to unify India under one rule. Though his inscriptions don't give the exact route of his conquests, we can get this information from the epic Raghuvaṃśa poem written by Kālidāsa. Kālidāsa was one of the nine jewels in the court of Emperor Yaśodharmā Viṣṇuvardhana Vikramāditya. Another famous personality among the nine jewels was the astronomer Varāhamihira. We have seen that Yaśodharmā was from Mandsaur, and Mandsaur was known as Daśapura in ancient times. It cannot be a coincidence that this small town called Daśapura is mentioned by Varāhamihira in Bṛhatsaṃhitā [12] and by Kālidāsa in Meghadūta [13]. Obviously, they had their patron Yaśodharmā Viṣṇuvardhana in mind while writing these texts.

Śrīrāma Goyala is of the opinion that Kālidāsa has written the account of the conquests of Raghu based on the route followed by Samudragupta [14]. However, this opinion is based on the faulty chronology. As Kālidāsa was a junior contemporary of Yaśodharmā, he did not have to look elsewhere for inspiration. According to the description of Raghu's conquests in Raghuvaṃśa [15], the route taken by Raghu was as follows [16-17]. He started by going eastward and conquering Suhma (West Bengal) and Vaṅga (South Bengal delta region). Utkala (North-eastern Odisha) was next followed by Kaliṅga (Southern Odisha, Eastern Telangana and Northern Andhra Pradesh). He continued south and crossed the Kaveri River. He then followed the eastern coast to the southern tip of India. On the way to the Malay mountain, the Pāṇḍya king paid his obeisance. He then turned northward to continue along the west coast. He crossed the Sahya Mountain and conquered the kingdoms on the west coast including Kerala. After continuing further, he turned west and conquered the Persians. Then Raghu turned north and went to the banks of Oxus and subdued the Hūṇas and Kambojas. He turned eastward again and conquered the kingdoms along the Himalayas, which included the Kirātas (inhabitants of Nepal) and Utsavasaṅketas (a tribe of the mountains who passed their lives in feasting and conviviality [18]). He then crossed the Lauhitya River and subdued the king of Prāgjyotiṣa/ Kāmarūpa (present day Assam). This is where the Digvijaya (global conquest) of Raghu was completed.

We have many similarities between this description and the conquests made by Yaśodharmā. Yaśodharmā has mentioned his conquests up to the Lauhitya River, which is also part of Raghu's conquests. Raghu conquered the Hūṇas, so did Yaśodharmā. Raghu conquered the regions along the Himalayas, so did Yaśodharmā. As Yaśodharmā mentions the Mahendra Mountain on the southern tip of India under his empire, he could have followed the same route that Raghu is supposed to have taken. Raghu's horses are supposed to have relieved their fatigue by rolling on the banks of the river Oxus. River Oxus is the Amu Darya in Central Asia, which was known as Vaṅkṣu in ancient India. On its banks was the kingdom of Bactria, modern day Balkh at the northern border of Afghanistan, close to Uzbekistan. In ancient India this area was known as Vāhlika and was often juxtaposed with Kambojas. We will now present evidence that Yaśodharmā had made conquests up to Vāhlika. The evidence comes from an inscription on the famous Delhi Iron pillar, which is located in the Qutb complex in Mehrauli.

Mehrauli is deformation of the original name of this locality, which was Mihirāwalī. It was named after the famous astronomer Varāhamihira. An astronomical complex was made here in honour of Varāhamihira, which consisted of twenty seven buildings, one for each nakṣatra (asterism). An iron pillar honouring the patron of Varāhamihira, Emperor Vikramāditya, was brought from Viṣṇupadagiri, and erected in this complex. In honour of Emperor Yaśodharmā Viṣṇuvardhana, the real Vikramāditya behind the legends, the pillar was named Viṣṇudhvaja as referred to in the last line of the Iron Pillar inscription. This astronomical complex was destroyed by invaders after the defeat of Prithvīrāj Chauhān towards the end of twelfth century CE, and a mosque called Quwwat-ul-Islam (Might of Islam) took its place. A still extant plaque outside the mosque, which was written by invaders soon after the destruction of the astronomical complex, proclaims that the mosque was made by destroying twenty seven temples. Number 27 is the key here, as this is the number of nakṣatras according to Hindu and Jain astronomy. As Hindus and Jains had adorned the astronomical complex with exquisite sculptures, this astronomical complex was mistaken as temples by the invaders. The inscription on the Mehrauli iron pillar has immortalized the fame of Vikramāditya Yaśodharmā Viṣṇuvardhana. It is quoted below for further discussion [19]:

> *"He, on whose arm fame was inscribed by the sword, when, in battle in the Vanga countries, he kneaded (and turned) back with (his) breast the enemies who, uniting together, came against (him); he, by whom, having crossed in warfare the seven mouths of the (river) Sindhu, the Vāhlikas were conquered; he, by the breezes of whose prowess the southern ocean is even still perfumed...*
>
> *(Line 3.) - He, the remnant of the great zeal of whose energy, which utterly destroyed (his) enemies, like (the remnant of the great glowing heat) of a burned-out fire in a great forest, even now leaves not the earth; though he, the king, as if wearied, has quitted this earth, and has gone to the other world, moving in (bodily) form to the land (of paradise) won by (the merit of has) actions, (but) remaining on (this) earth by (the memory of his) fame...*
>
> *(L. 5.) - By him, the king, who attained sole supreme sovereignty in the world, acquired by his own arm and (enjoyed) for a very long time; (and) who, having the name of Chandra, carried a beauty of countenance like (the beauty of) the full-moon, having in faith fixed his mind upon (the god) Viṣṇu, this lofty standard of the divine Viṣṇu was set up on the hill (called) Viṣṇupada."*

The use of word Viṣṇu three times in the last sentence reinforces the conclusion that this iron pillar commemorates the victories of Vikramāditya Yaśodharmā Viṣṇuvardhana. Historians have various theories about the identity of the king mentioned in this inscription. Most of them have focused on kings having the name Chandra, such as Chandragupta Maurya, Chandrāṃśa,

Sadāchandra, Chandravarmā, Chandragupta-I, and Chandragupta II [20]. Śrīrāma Goyala has identified this king with Samudragupta, as he considers him to be the only king who had made extensive conquests justifying this identification [21]. However, Vikramāditya Yaśodharmā Viṣṇuvardhana fulfills this criterion better. His association with Varāhamihira and naming of the locality Mehrauli after Varāhamihira seals this identification. The only objection to this identification is the name Chandra for the king in this inscription. Chandra (moon) in this inscription refers to the name of the dynasty of Yaśodharmā Viṣṇuvardhana, which was Aulikara. Here is the opinion of noted historian D. C. Sircar regarding the meaning of Aulikara [22]:

> *"The real meaning of auli is uncertain; sometimes aulikara is interpreted as himakara or the moon."*

Vikramāditya Yaśodharmā was not only a great warrior, but also a great patron of learning. His court was adorned with very talented people from all fields of knowledge. Nine of them were most notable and were called the nine gems of his court. An astrological text, Jyotirvidābharaṇa, gives the name of the nine gems in the court of Vikramāditya. Jyotirvidābharaṇa is supposedly written by Kālidāsa, but modern historians consider this text to be a forgery. Bhāo Dājī has given the following information about Vikramāditya from the text Jyotirvidābharaṇa [23]:

> *"The conclusion to the Jyotirvidābharaṇa, which contains the verse respecting the "nine gems" so frequently quoted as a "memorial verse" without any one having been able to trace it to source, is given entire below, as the author enters into chronological details regarding himself not met with in any of the well known works of the great Kālidāsa.*
>
> *Translation of Chapter 22, containing twenty-one verses.*
>
> *1. I now proceed to give in order the subjects already treated of, and to describe the joy producing monarch, Vikrama.*

[The 2nd to the 6th verse contains the names of the subjects, and the 6th verse states that the total number of verses in the book are 1,424, and that the book is named "Jyotirvidābharaṇa Kāyva."]

7. By me has this work been produced in the reign of Vikrama over Mālava in Bhārata Varsha, which is rendered delightful by the study of the Śrutis and Smṛtis, and which contains 180 countries.

8. Śaṅku, Vararuchi, Maṇi, Anśudatta, Jishṇu, Trilochana, Hari, Ghaṭakharpara, also Amara Sinha and other poets, adorned his assembly.

9. Satya, Varāha Mihira, Śrita Sena, Śrī Bādarāyaṇa, Maṇittha, and Kumāra Sinha, were the astronomers, and myself and other professors of astronomy also.

10. Dhanwantari, Kṣapaṇaka, Amarasinha, Śaṅku, Vetālabhaṭṭa, Ghaṭakharpara, Kālidāsa, the renowned Varāha Mihira and Vararuchi, are the nine gems of Vikrama.

11. Vikrama flourished, and at his court attended 800 Mandalika (minor) Rajas; and at the great assembly there were 16 eloquent pundits, 10 astronomers, 6 physicians, and 16 reciters of the Vedas.

12. His army occupied 18 yojanas of ground; his forces consisted of 3 crores of infantry, 10 crores of cavalry, 24,300 elephants, and 400,000 boats. No monarch could be compared to him.

13. He celebrated his victory over the world by the destruction of ninety-five Śaka chiefs, and established his era in the Kaliyuga; and by daily giving in alms, pearls, gold, jewels, cows, horses and elephants, he brightened the face of Dharma.

14. He destroyed the proud king of Dravida, also the king of Lāṭa, defeated the king of Gauda, and conquered him of Gurjaradeśa, removed the darkness of Dhārā, delighted the king of Kamboja, and conducted himself with success.

15. His prowess and qualities were like those of Indra, Ambhodhī, Amaradru, Smara and Meru. He was the delight of his subjects, and humbled his enemies by conquering and restoring their forts to them.

16. He protects the capital Ujjayinī, the great city which gives beatitude to its inhabitants, and which is celebrated for the presence of Mahākāla.

17. In a great battle he conquered the king of the Śakas in Ruma, paraded his royal prisoner in Ujjayinī, and afterwards set him free. Such was his irresistible prowess.

18. Whilst Vikrama thus reigned in Avanti, the people enjoyed prosperity, happiness, and wealth, and the injunctions of the Vedas were everywhere observed.

19. Śaṅku and many other pundits and poets, and Varāha Mihira and other astronomers, flourished at his court. They respect the genius of me, who am a friend of the king.

20. Having first composed three Kāvyas, i.e. the Raghuvanśa and others, I composed several treatises on Vedic subjects (Śriti Karmavāda); then from Kālidāsa proceeded the astrological treatise called Jyotirvidābharaṇa.

21. 3068 years of Kali having passed, in the month of Vyśākha I commenced composing the work, and completed it in the month of Kārtika. Having zealously examined many astronomical works, I have composed this treatise for the edification of astronomers."

Though the authenticity of Jyotirvidābharaṇa has been questioned, it should be kept in mind that even according to colonial historians this text was written long before British came to India. The information contained in these verses was believed to be true when Jyotirvidābharaṇa was written. These verses provide us with a wealth of information about the most endearing monarch of ancient India.

A major point is the specification of the place where the epic battle was fought between Vikrāmāditya Yaśodharmā and the Śaka ruler Mihirakula. This battle was fought in Rumā, which is near Sambhar Lake between Ajmer and Jaipur in Rajasthan. This place is about 400 km north of Mandsaur, and fits the description of the area where the battle could have been fought, if we keep in mind that Mihirakula entered India through the plains of Punjab and had extended his rule up to Gwalior in Madhya Pradesh, which is about 400 km east of Rumā. As Yaśodharmā's family was ruling from Mandsaur to begin with, and Mihirakula had taken over most of the area north of Yaśodharmā's kingdom, a battle between them in Rumā implies that Yaśodharmā had initiated the battle by taking his forces up north in Mihirakula's territory. We should keep in mind that Mihirakula was a barbarian foreigner (mlechchha) and getting rid of mlechchhas was an honourable duty of Indian kings. After the battle, Mihirakula was held captive and paraded in Ujjayinī before being set free. This is consistent with Yaśodharmā's inscription in which it is said that Mihirakula had to bow his head at Yaśodharmā's feet, but nothing is said about executing him.

We next come to the nine gems in Vikrāmāditya's court. Verse 10 of Chapter 22 of Jyotirvidābharaṇa gives the names of nine gems in the court of emperor Vikrāmāditya -- Dhanwantari, Kṣapaṇaka, Amarasiṃha, Śaṅku, Vetālabhaṭṭa, Ghaṭakarpara, Kālidāsa, Varāhamihira and Vararuchi. These nine celebrities were the most noted in the court of Vikrāmāditya among many more luminaries such as Maṇi, Anśudatta, Jiṣṇu, Trilochana, Hari, Satya, Śrita Sena, Śrī Bādarāyaṇa, Maṇittha, and Kumāra Sinha.

The tradition of nine gems or Navaratna is engrained in the collective memory of the Hindus. Even Akbar tried to duplicate it after he came to know of it. Before him, king Bhoja is also supposed to have had nine gems in his court. There exists a short text called Navaratna, which was written to preserve this tradition.

Goonetilleke has provided us with the following information about this text and the prevailing wisdom of the time in the nineteenth century as follows [24]:

> *"For a very long period after the discovery of Sanskrit, the Navaratna remained unknown to European Orientalists, and even at the present day it appears that what is known of it is almost nothing beyond the fact of its existence in Ceylon in manuscript, with a Sinhalese translation and commentary, and even this scanty information is confined to a very small minority of Western scholars.*
>
> *If the importance of a literary work is to be judged by its length alone, or, in other words, if its extent is the only point to be taken into account, when its worth has to be considered, the Navaratna certainly could not lay claim to that attention which the generality of Sanskrit works have met with at the hands of the learned; for the entire work, excluding the translation and commentary, is ridiculously short, consisting as it does of only eleven stanzas, ... Of these eleven stanzas, the first two are introductory. The remaining nine, which constitute the body of the book, are not the work of one single author, but the independent compositions of nine different sages, who were contemporaries and formed the chief ornaments of the court of one art-loving sovereign who is known by the title of Vikrama or Vikrāmāditya.*
>
> *The two introductory verses, of which one gives the names of the nine authors and the other the first words of their compositions, are intended to serve as a help or key to recall to mind the nine stanzas, and to ascertain, without referring to the book, the author of each one of them. This object has been accomplished by arranging the names of the authors, the first words of the stanzas and the stanzas themselves in corresponding order. The first introductory verse is as follows:*
>
> DhanwantariKṣapaṇakāmarasiṃhaŚaṅku-
> VetālabhaṭṭaGhaṭakarparaKālidāsāḥ |

Khyāto Varāhamihiro Nṛpateḥ Sabhāyām
Ratnāni vai Vararuchirnava Vikramasya ||"

"Dhanwantari, Kṣapaṇaka, Amarasiṃha, Śaṅku, Vetālabhaṭṭa, Ghaṭakarpara, Kālidāsa, the celebrated Varāhamihira and Vararuchi are indeed, the nine gems of the court of king Vikrama."

Although European Orientalists were not made aware of the existence of the Navaratna until a comparatively recent date, they, in one way or another, became acquainted with this verse at an early period of their researches into Sanskrit literature - not, indeed, as a stanza of a book, but as one transmitted orally through several succeeding generations from remote antiquity down to the present time.

Judging from the statements which they have made regarding it and which will presently be quoted, I am inclined to believe that they heard it freely repeated by Brahmans, who, like all other Orientalists, are in the habit of repeating stanzas to while away their time when no business engagements keep them occupied. The reciters must have known, however, that it was the 'first introductory verse of the Navaratna - the work being known in India as well as in Ceylon, as will be shown in the sequel - but they probably had reasons of their own for concealing this fact from their European friends, or it may have been that these European scholars came to the conclusion at which they arrived without giving the matter the necessary consideration.

Bentley, who always entertained the greatest contempt for Hindu learning, and who literally abused Colebrooke and others for vindicating such studies, appears to have been the first to discover the verse. Anxious as he always was to grasp every bit of information which would afford him some argument against the value of the arts and sciences of the Hindus, he wielded - as he thought - in this verse a powerful weapon for demolishing what in his opinion was the pretended antiquity of the astronomical systems of the Hindus.

Professor H. Wilson, in the preface to the first edition of his Sanskrit dictionary, refutes Bentley's arguments, and for that purpose enters upon a consideration of the value to be attached to the verse. He speaks of it as being simply traditional, and not found in any known work, with the probable exception of a work called the Vikramacaritra. He adds that no reliance can be placed on the authenticity of the verse, as it mentions "Ghaṭakarpara" as the name of a man, whereas in point of fact, it is that of a work, and he winds up by saying that the arguments of Bentley must fall to the ground, as they are based upon the assumption that the verse in question is authentic and genuine.

Loiseleur Deslongehamps, a French author, refers to the verse in the preface to his Amarakosa published in 1839 as an ancient tradition, and one universally prevalent in India ... He agrees with Wilson in the supposition that Ghaṭakarpara was the name of a poem, and in his surmise that the verse is to be found in the Vikramacaritra, but Professor Albrecht Weber, who will be presently referred to again, says that it is not given in the Vikramacaritra, and that Ghaṭakarpara is the name of a man to whom several poems are ascribed. ...

Hippolyte Fauche, another French author, in an article headed "..." characterises the verse as a mnemonic verse, of which the source and date of authorship are equally unknown ...

Dr. H. Kern, in the preface to his edition of the Brihatsaṃhitā, written in 1863, says that it is a memorial verse and that it is in the mouth of every Pundit, and was so half a century ago, referring no doubt to the time of Bentley.

Albrecht Weber, whom we have already referred to, in his Akademische Vorlesungen, p. 218, calls it a memorial verse (denkverse) and adds that we could say of it, as of the maid from the foreign country that nobody knew from whence it came ...

Later on, European Orientalists discovered that the verse was found in an astrological work called the Jyotirvidābharaṇa. This fact, however, rather than raising their estimation of it as an authentic declaration of a true historical event, had quite a contrary effect. There were several reasons for regarding the Jyotirvidābharaṇa as a work of no importance whatever. I have not seen it, but Dr. Kern, who has read it and carefully examined it, is very strong in his condemnation of it as a downright forgery. He says that the author of this production is "an impostor, and a very clumsy one, so that his word cannot carry much weight." It would be tedious to notice all his arguments for the opinion he has formed, but they appear to be sound and conclusive. Such indeed is the contempt with which the book was regarded that one writer, F. E. Hall, has assailed the verse in question on the sole ground that it is found in such a worthless book and one of such modern date as the Jyotirvidābharaṇa.

Later on still, Westergaard, a Danish Orientalist, discovered the existence of the Navaratna in Ceylon, and the fact that the verse in question was found in it. He inserted the work in his Catalogue of Sanskrit MSS and after him Aufrecht inserted it in his. From these two sources Albrecht Weber became acquainted with these facts, but he does not appear to have read or even seen the Navaratna. He was also aware that the verse was found in the Jyotirvidābharaṇa, which in his opinion is a work of about the 16th century, but his view of the matter is that the origin of the verse is not to be sought for in either of these works, the authors of which must have, according to him, simply reduced to writing and thus rescued from oblivion the verse which existed long before their time in the oral literature of the Hindus. I gather this from the use of the word "aufgenommen" in the following sentence, in which he speaks of both the Jyotirvidābharaṇa and the Navaratna …

We now come to the questions arising for consideration from a perusal of the stanza. These are, first, were the nine gems mentioned in it actually contemporaries? And, secondly, Who was the king Vikrama in whose court they are said to have flourished?

Before entering upon these questions, I think it necessary to give a brief account of those of the nine gems of whom any knowledge has been preserved down to our times. These are Dhanvantari, Amarasiṃha, Kālidāsa, Varāhamihira, and Vararuchi. Little, if not absolutely nothing, is known of the remaining four, viz., Ksapaṇaka, Śaṅku, Vetālabhaṭṭa, and Ghaṭakarpara.

Dhanvantari was a famous physician, and the author of a dictionary of materia medica, called the Dhanvantari-nighaṇṭa. He was the tutor of Śuśruta, whose celebrated medical work is held in high estimation all over India, and has recently been introduced into Ceylon. It has superseded almost all the former medical works used in the island, and now engages the attention of Sinhalese medical students.

Amarasiṃha is also called Amaradeva, or simply Amara. The first of these names Amarasiṃha would make it very probable that he belonged to the Kṣatriya or military caste, while the second, Amaradeva, would incline us to the belief that he was a Brāhman. He is by general repute said to have been a Buddhist, although some of his scholiasts deny this statement as unsupported by evidence.

He was the founder of one of the eight principal schools of Sanskrit grammar, as will be seen from a verse of Vopadeva's to be quoted in the sequel, and was besides the author of a Sanskrit dictionary of nouns and particles, called the "Amarakoṣa," the treasure of Amara, which is regarded as of the highest authority, and is copiously quoted by Mallinātha and other commentators of Sanskrit works. Being in verse it is committed to memory by native Sanskrit scholars, who thereby make themselves acquainted with nearly all the words in the Sanskrit language except roots. The Abidhānappadipikā and the Nāmāvaliya, which have been edited and published in Ceylon by two learned scholars, Vaskaḍuve Subhūti Terunnānse and the Rev. C. Alwis, respectively, are composed on the model of the Amarakoṣa and are to the Pāli and Sinhalese what the Amarakoṣa is to the Sanskrit. ***It is also the work which afforded a hint to Roget in the composition of his own "Thesaurus," and even in the title which he gives to that work - the Sanskrit Koṣa and the Latin Thesaurus, both meaning treasure.***

The Amarakoṣa was brought to Ceylon, and translated into Sinhalese several centuries ago. The Sinhalese translation is accompanied by an excellent commentary, and the work together with this translation and commentary exists even at the present day, when most of the Sanskrit books imported to the island have either been lost or become exceedingly rare.

I shall not dwell further on this work as I shall have occasion in a future article to speak of it, or rather of its Sinhalese version and commentary as falling quite within the province of the heading of this paper. We now come to Kālidāsa. He was a poet of the first order, and such of his works as have come down to us have enabled us to form some idea of the depth of thought and the fertility of poetical imagination which characterised the Hindū mind at the time of its authorship. A description of all his works would swell out this paper to a very inconvenient length. I shall, therefore, content myself with merely giving them here a passing notice.

One of these works is the " Raghuvaṃśa," or the "Race of the Raghus," a poem narrating the history and exploits of several princes of this race, who were descended from Manu, surnamed Vaivasvata, the first of the kings of the earth, and of whom Rāma, the hero of the Rāmāyaṇa and an incarnation of Vishnu, was the most celebrated. ...

Another work of Kālidāsa is the "Ṛtu-saṃhāra,"assemblage of the seasons." There is an interesting fact always remembered in connection with this work, namely, that it is the first book ever printed in Sanskrit. It was printed in 1792 under the auspices of Sir Wm. Jones, and the following advertisement to the work will, I think, be read with much interest by Sanskritists of the present day:

"This book is the first ever printed in Sanskrit; and it is by the press alone that the ancient literature of India can long be preserved; a learner of that most interesting language, who had carefully perused one of the popular grammars, could hardly begin his course of study with an easier or more elegant work than the Ritusanhara, or assemblage of the seasons. Every line composed by Kālidāsa is exquisitely polished, and every couplet in the following poem exhibits an Indian landscape, always beautiful, sometimes highly coloured, but never beyond nature. Four copies of it have been diligently collated, and where they differed, the clearest and most natural reading has constantly had the preference."

The Kumārasambhava, the birth of Kumāra, the god of war, the Nalodaya, the history of king Nala, the Meghadūta, the cloud messenger, and the Śṛṅgāratilaka, the tilaka of love, are also poems by Kālidāsa. Besides these he was the author of two dramatic works, called the Śakuntalā and the Vikramorvaśī, as well as of a treatise on prosody, called the Śrutabodha.

The German authors especially are great admirers of Kālidāsa. Speaking of the Śakuntalā, Augustus Wilhelm von Schlegel says:-

> *"Among the Indians, the people from whom perhaps all the cultivation of the human race has been derived, plays were known long before they could have experienced any foreign influence. The only specimen of their plays (nāṭakas) hitherto known to us, is the delightful Śakuntalā, which, notwithstanding the colouring of a foreign climate, bears in its general structure a striking resemblance to our romantic drama."*

Alexander von Humboldt, in treating of Indian poetry observes:-

"Kālidāsa, the celebrated author of the Śakuntalā, is a masterly describer of the influence which nature exercises upon the minds of lovers. Tenderness in the expression of feeling, and richness of creative fancy have assigned to him his lofty place among the poets of all nations." ...

The learned sage mentioned immediately after Kālidāsa is Varāhamihira, also culled Varāhamihara, who is distinguished in the verse by the epithet "Khyāta," "celebrated," and who in reality was one of the greatest, if not the greatest, of all Hindū astronomers. ...

His first astronomical work, called the Pañchasiddhāntikā, is lost beyond all hope of recovery, and is known at present only from quotations in other authors.

He is the author also of several other works on the different branches of the astronomical and astrological science of the Hindus, of which the Bṛhat-saṃhitā is the most celebrated. It is now-a-days but little studied, owing perhaps to the want of encouragement given to such studies by the princes of India, whose palmy days have long since passed away. ...

The last of the nine gems is Vararuchi, a poet, grammarian, lexicographer, and a writer on medicine. He was also the author of the Prākṛt Grammar called Prākṛt-prakāśa, which has been edited and published with the commentary of Bhāmaha, and with copious notes and an English translation by Edward Byles Cowell. Vararuchi is also said to be the first grammarian who reduced the various dialects of Prākṛt to a system. He is sometimes identified with Kātyāyana, the author of the Vārttikas to Pāṇini's Sūtras."

There are many points to note from this paper. First, we have conclusive evidence that the tradition of nine gems in the court of Vikramāditya is a very well-established tradition. It was considered so sacrosanct that it was memorized from generation to generation using mnemonics. Second, the evidence of Jyotirvidābharaṇa is so damning to the accepted chronology that colonial historians went hammer and tongs at it to discredit it. Whether it was written in 33 BCE by Kālidāsa or someone else claiming to be Kālidāsa several centuries later, since it was written before the arrival of Europeans in India, the traditions described in it genuinely represent what was believed by Hindus and Jains for centuries.

The evidence of Varāhamihira has been misused to discredit the whole tradition. We have shown in "India before Alexander: A New Chronology" that Varāhamihira indeed lived in the first century BCE. In this chapter, we have now shown that there indeed was an emperor Vikramāditya in the first century BCE, whose empire not only included most of current day India, Bangladesh and Pakistan, but extended up to Bactria of yesteryears. There should be no reason now to doubt the authenticity of the tradition of nine gems of emperor Vikramāditya. We have read about five of the nine gems -- Dhanvantari, Amarasiṃha, Kālidāsa, Varāhamihira, and Vararuchi -- in the paper by Goonetilleke above. At this point, we would like to point out that there is also inscriptional evidence for Amarasiṃha being in the court of emperor Vikramāditya during the first century BCE as follows [25]:

> *"An inscription found by Mr. Wilkins at Buddha Gayā, of which he published a translation in Asiatic Researches (I, 284), and which was written to commemorate the foundation of a temple of Buddha by Amara Siṃha, bears the date 1005 of the era of Vikramāditya, answering to the Christian year 949: the authenticity of this inscription we have no reason to question, as it professes no object to which suspicion of fraud or interest can be attached, and it is perfectly consistent with the character and traditions of the place in which it was found: the identity of the person is also indisputable, as all ancient authorities concur in representing Amara as a worshipper of Buddha, and he is designated in the inscription in the usual manner as one of the nine gems of Vikramāditya's court. ... The author states that his having derived his knowledge of Amara's being the founder of the temple from its records, or as it is translated "from the authority of the place", an authority which no doubt existed, as most celebrated shrines are furnished with a legend, a*

lying one it may be granted, which professes to give their history: and it matters not here, of what description was the record of the temple of Buddhas, as, if in the middle of the tenth century it had converted Amara Sinha into the hero of a holy fable, it at least proves his prior and remote existence.

To return to the inscription: the writer states that "Amara was the favourite and minister of Vikramāditya, who was certainly a king renowned in the world", and whom he intends by Vikramāditya can scarcely be doubted, as he dates from that prince's era: it is therefore perfectly clear that at so distant a period as A.D. 949, if the inscription is to be trusted, the same traditional account of Amara's date prevailed, which is still received, and however accurate or incorrect this tradition may have been, its existence is fatal to the supposition that the subject of it was alive at the period when such a belief was current, and still more so to the opinion we have noticed of his flourishing at some subsequent date.

That the inscription is worthy of credit, I see no reason to doubt, and it is assuredly an authority of more weight than the notions of nameless Paṇḍits, the sole impugners of the belief it sanctions."

Let us see if there is anything known about the remaining four gems -- Kṣapaṇaka, Śaṅku, Vetālabhaṭṭa, and Ghaṭakharpara. Monier-Williams' Sanskrit-English dictionary gives information about three of them -- Kṣapaṇaka, Vetālabhaṭṭa, and Ghaṭakharpara. Kṣapaṇaka means a religious mendicant, typically a Jain mendicant, who wears no garments, and was perhaps the Jain astronomer Siddhasena [26]. Vetālabhaṭṭa was a poet and author of Nīti-pradīpa [27]. Ghaṭakharpara was a poet, who wrote a poem named after him, and was also the author of Nīti-sāra [28]. Śaṅku is considered to be an architect [29] or a poet and educationist [30].

We now have a picture of an emperor par excellence, whose court was filled with learned people from all walks of life. He was a great patron of learning and his generosity was legendary. As India suffered under the attacks of the barbarians one after another, the fascination with emperor Vikramāditya grew. It became the stuff of legends – of an emperor who had chased the barbarians all the way to Bactria. Over time, he became the hero of a number of fables, as described in the Vetālapañchaviṃśati (popularly known as Vetāla Pachīsī), Siṃhāsana-dwātṛṃśikā (popularly known as Siṃhāsana Battīsī), and Śuka-saptaśatī (popularly known as the story of a Parrot and a Mynah). In the popular imagination, Vikramāditya was a paragon of virtue, a just ruler, a generous king, and a warrior par excellence.

As described in the Delhi Iron Pillar inscription, Vikramāditya Yaśodharmā enjoyed life for a long time, and when he passed away in 57 BCE at an advanced age, an era came to an end. The people of India instituted the Vikrama era to preserve his memory. It is the testimony of their love that the Vikrama era continues to be in use even today. Even though Emperor Vikramāditya Yaśodharmā left this world more than 2000 years ago, Indians continue to cherish his memory.

We will continue with the reconstruction of the history of India in the next book in this series, "India after Vikramaditya", which will present a radically different picture than the one currently believed.

Notes

1. Fleet (1888): 90.
2. Goyala (1987a): 338.
3. Fleet (1888): 160-161.
4. Saloman (1989).
5. Rājataraṅgiṇī 1.310.
6. Fleet (1888): 163-164.
7. Fleet (1888): 154-158.
8. Fleet (1888): 147-148.
9. Majumdar and Altekar (1967): 197-198.
10. Beal (1884):165-172.
11. Fleet (1888): 93.
12. Bṛhatsaṃhitā XIV.2
13. Meghadūta 1.49. (Daśapura Vadhūnetra kautūhalānām)
14. Goyala (1987b): 264-265.
15. Raghuvaṃśa 4.32-84.
16. Goyala (1987b): 264-265.
17. Gopal (1984): 59-60.
18. Duncker (1880): 428.
19. Fleet (1888): 141-142.
20. Goyala (1987b): 48-49.
21. Goyala (1987b): 50-56.
22. Sircar (1966): 37.
23. Dājī (1861).
24. Goonetilleke (1884).
25. Rost (1865): 180-182.
26. Monier-Williams (1988): 326.
27. Monier-Williams (1988): 1015.
28. Monier-Williams (1988): 375.
29. Chatterjee (1998): 223.
30. Nirmala (1992): 131.

BIBLIOGRAPHY

Agrawal, A. (1989). Rise and Fall of the Imperial Guptas. New Delhi, India: Motilal Banarsidass.

Anson, E. M. (2013). Alexander the Great: Themes and issues. London, UK: Bloomsbury Academic.

Basham, A.L. (1982). Aśoka and Buddhism – A Reexamination. The Journal of the International Association of Buddhistic Studies, 5 (1): 131-143.

Bakshi, S. R. and Ralhan, O. P. (editors). (2007). Madhya Pradesh Through the Ages. Volume 3. Delhi, India: Sarup and Sons.

Beal, S. (1884). Si-Yu-Ki: Buddhist Records of the Western World, Volume I. London, UK: Trubner and Co.

Beal, S. (1906). Si-Yu-Ki: Buddhist Records of the Western World, Volume I. London, UK: Kegan Paul, Trench, Trubner and Co Ltd.

Burgess, J. (1878). Report on the Antiquities in the Bidar and Aurangabad Districts, in the territories of his highness the Nizam of Haidarabad, being the result of the third season's operations of the Archaeological Survey of Western India, 1875-76. London, UK: W. H. Allen and Co.

Chatterjee, S. (1998). Indian Civilization and Culture. New Delhi, India: M D Publications Pvt Ltd.

Chinnock, E. J. (1884). The Anabasis of Alexander. London, UK: Hodder and Stoughton.

Colebrooke, H.T. (1873). Miscellaneous Essays. Volume 3. London, UK: Trubner & Co.

Cunningham, A. (1883). Book of Indian Eras, with Tables for calculating Indian Dates. London, UK: Thacker, Spink and Co.

Dājī, B. (1861). On the Sanskrit Poet, Kālidāsa. Journal of the Bombay Branch of the Royal Asiatic Society, 21: 19-30.

Dāji, B. (1872). The Inroads of the Scythians into India, and the Story of Kālakāchārya. Journal of the Asiatic Society of Bombay, Volume IX, 1867-1870: 139-146.

Duncker, M. (1880). The History of Antiquity. Volume 4. London, UK: Richard Bentley & Son.

Falk, H. (2001). The yuga of Sphujiddhvaja and the era of the Kuṣāṇas. Silk Road Art and Archaeology, 7, 121-136.

Falk, H. (2004). The Kaniṣka Era in Gupta Records. Silk Road Art and Archaeology, 10, 167-176.

Falk, H. and Bennett, C. (2009). Macedonian Intercalary Months and the Era of Azes. Acta Orientalia, 70, 197-216.

Fleet, J. F. (1888). Corpus Inscriptionum Indicarum, Vol. III: Inscriptions of the Early Guptas. Calcutta, India: Government of India, Central Publications Branch.

Goonetilleke, W. (1884). The Navaratna. The Orientalist, 1: 97-109.

Gopal, R. (1984). Kālidāsa: His Art and Culture. New Delhi, India: Concept Publishing Company.

Goyala, S. (1987a). Gupta Sāmrājya kā Itihāsa (in Hindi). Meerut, U.P., India: Kusumāñjali Prakāśana.

Goyala, S. (1987b). Samudragupta Parākramāṅka (in Hindi). Meerut, U.P., India: Kusumāñjali Prakāśana.

Hamilton, H. C. (1892). The Geography of Strabo. Volume 1. London, UK: George Bell and Sons.

Jain, K. C. (1972). Malwa Through the Ages. New Delhi, India: Motilal Banarsidass.

Jarrett, H.S. (1891). Ain-I-Akbari by Abul Fazl Allami, Vol. II, Book 3. Calcutta, India: Asiatic Society of Bengal.

Kumar, V., Sreenadh, O., and Hegde, S. G. (2013). Lagna Varahi (by Varahamihira). India: Ancient Indian Astrology Foundation.

Konow, S. (1923). Acta Orientalia, 1: 14-26, as quoted by Sethna, K. D. (1989). Ancient India in a New Light. New Delhi, India: Aditya Prakashana, page 474.

Majumdar, R. C. and Altekar, A. S. (editors). (1967). The Vakataka-Gupta Age. , Delhi, India: Motilal Banarasidass.

Majumdar, R.C., Pusalker, A.D. and Majumdar A.K. (Editors). (2001). The History and Culture of the Indian People, Volume II: The Age of Imperial Unity. 7th Edition. Mumbai, India: Bharatiya Vidya Bhavan.

Malla, K. P. (2005). Manadeva Samvat: An investigation into an Historical Fraud. Contributions to Nepalese Studies, 32 (1): 1-49.

McCrindle, J. W. (1893). The Invasion of India by Alexander the Great. Westminster, UK: Archibald Constable and Co.

McCrindle, J. W. (1901). Ancient India as Described in Classical Literature. Westminster, UK: Archibald Constable and Co.

Mirashi, V.V. (editor). (1963). Corpus Inscriptionum Indicarum, Vol. V, Inscriptions of the Vākāṭakas. New Delhi, India: Archaeological Survey of India.

Mirashi, V.V. (1974). Bhavabhūti: His Date, Life, and Works. Delhi, India: Motilal Banarsidass.

Monier-Williams, M. (1988). Sanskrit-English dictionary. Third reprint. New Delhi, India: Munshiram Manoharlal.

Mookerji, R., (1973). The Gupta Empire. Fifth Edition. New Delhi, India: Motilal Banarsidass.

Nirmala, R. (1992). Anādi Ujjayinī (in Hindi). Mumbai, India: Anviti Prakāśana.

Pandey, R. B., (1951). Vikramāditya of Ujjayinī. Banaras, India: Shatadala Prakashana.

Pargiter, F. E. (1913). The Purana Text of the Dynasties of the Kali Age. London, UK: Humphrey Milford and Oxford University Press.

Penzer, N.M. (editor) (1928). The Ocean of Story: Being C.H. Tawney's translation of Somadeva's Katha Sarit Sagara. Volume 9. London, UK: Chas. J. Sawyer Ltd.

Rao, N. L. (1931-32). Gokak plates of Dejja-Maharaja. Epigraphia Indica, 21: 289-292.

Rost, R. (editor) (1865). Essays: Analytical, Critical and Philological on the subjects connected with Sanskrit literature by the late H.H. Wilson. Volume 3. London, UK: Trubner & Co.

Roy, R. R. M. (2015). India before Alexander: A New Chronology. Mississauga, Ontario, Canada: Mount Meru Publishing.

Sachau, E. C. (1910a). Alberuni's India. Vol. 1. London, UK: Kegan Paul, Trench, Trubner & Co. Ltd.

Sachau, E. C. (1910b). Alberuni's India. Vol. 2. London, UK: Kegan Paul, Trench, Trubner & Co. Ltd.

Saloman, R. (1989). New Inscriptional Evidence for the History of the Aulikaras of Mandasor. Indo-Iranian Journal, 32: 1-36.

Saloman, R. (1998). Indian Epigraphy. New York, USA: Oxford University Press.

Sethna, K. D. (1989). Ancient India in a New Light. New Delhi, India: Aditya Prakashana.

Sircar, D.C. (1965). Indian Epigraphy. First edition. Delhi, India: Motilal Banarsidass.

Sircar, D.C. (1966). Indian Epigraphical Glossary. Delhi, India: Motilal Banarsidass.

Sircar, D.C. (1969). Ancient Malwā and the Vikramāditya Tradition. Delhi, India: Munshiram Manoharlal.

Smith, V. A. (1915). The Oxford Student's History of India, 5th Edition. London, UK: Clarendon Press.

Srinivasan, D. M. (2007). On the Cusp of an Era. Leiden, Netherlands: Brill.

Sule, A., Vahia, M., Joglekar, H., and Bhujle, S. (2007). Saptarṣi's visit to different Nakshatras: Subtle effect of Earth's precession. Indian Journal of History of science, 42(2): 133-147.

Thapar, R. (2003). The Penguin History of Early India: From the origins to AD 1300. New Delhi, India: Penguin Book.

van der Waerden, B. L.. (1980). The conjunction of 3102 B.C. Centaurus, 24: 117-131.

Venkatachelam, K. (1953). The plot in Indian Chronology. Ghandhinagara/Vijayawada, India: Bharata Charitra Bhaskara.

Vyāsa, R. (Editor). (1990). Saṃvat-pravarttaka Samrāṭa Vikramāditya (in Hindi). Delhi, India: Pāṇḍulipi Prakāśana.

Wilford, C. (1809a). Essay III: Of the kings of Magadha; their chronology. Asiatic Researches, 9: 82-116.

Wilford, C. (1809b). Essay IV: Vicramaditya and Salivahana. Asiatic Researches, 9: 117-243.

Willis, M. (2005). Later Gupta History: Inscriptions, Coins and Historical Ideology. Journal of the Royal Asiatic Society, Third Series, 15(2), 131-150.

INDEX

ABOUT THE AUTHOR

Dr. Raja Ram Mohan Roy earned his undergraduate degree in Metallurgical Engineering from Indian Institute of Technology, Kanpur and Ph.D. in Materials Science and Engineering from The Ohio State University, USA. He moved to Canada as a Postdoctoral Fellow. Raja has conducted research and development in the areas of Extractive Metallurgy and Materials Processing for twenty years. He has co-authored 40 research papers that have been published in peer-reviewed journals and proceedings of international symposia. He has co-edited the book "Innovative Process Development in Metallurgical Industry."

Raja has always had a fascination for ancient Indian civilization. Through his writings, Raja hopes to contribute towards the continuity and understanding of his civilization and, in the Indic tradition, repay the debt to his ancestors for their contributions and their sacrifices.

www.ingramcontent.com/pod-product-compliance
Lightning Source LLC
Chambersburg PA
CBHW051824040426
42447CB00006B/350